# FREEING THE PRISONERS

A SPECULATIVE FICTION NOVELLA

THE NEXT HIGH PRIEST SERIES
BOOK 5

PETER DEHAAN

*Freeing the Prisoners: A Speculative Fiction Novella*

Copyright © 2025 by Peter DeHaan

The Next High Priest Series, Book 5.

Library of Congress Control Number: 2024927587

Published by Rock Rooster Books, Grand Rapids, Michigan

**ISBNs:**

- 979-8-88809-124-1 (ebook)
- 979-8-88809-125-8 (paperback)
- 979-8-88809-126-5 (audiobook)

**Credits:**

- Developmental editor: Julie Harbison

- Copyeditor: Robyn Mulder
- Cover design: Fanderclai Design
- Author photo: Chelsie Jensen Photography

*To all who seek freedom from their prisons. May you secure your release.*

# CONTENTS

Freeing the Prisoners                          1
1. A New Day Dawns                             2
2. Rescued                                     6
3. Conflict                                   12
4. Grace                                      19
5. Reconciling                               26
6. The Plan                                   33
7. Missing                                    39
8. Road Trip                                  44
9. Direction                                  51
10. A Formidable Challenge                    58
11. Action at Last                            65
12. Found                                     74
13. Lost                                      79
14. We Must Leave                             84
15. Away                                      91
16. Provisions                                96
17. Time to Grieve?                          103
18. Interviewed                              107
19. Testimony                                116
20. Parting Words                            123
21. Leaving at Last                          127
22. Heading Home                             132
23. An Eventful Trip                         137
24. Celebrate                                144
Fighting the Fanatics                        153

*About Peter DeHaan*                161

*Fiction Books by Peter DeHaan*        163

# FREEING THE PRISONERS

**In a world just like ours . . . only different.**

*Free the prisoners, heal the sick, wake the dead, and proclaim
the Sovereign throughout all the nations.* -Prophecy 17.3

# 1

## A NEW DAY DAWNS

Emma basked in the afterglow of the Sovereign's work at yesterday's Sunday services. She greeted the morning with an unusual perkiness, full of expectation for her work at the Temple. Her progress in leading the people into a deeper relationship with the Almighty thrilled her. It was going to be a great day—at least that's what she prayed.

With an hour before school, she strolled to the Temple cafeteria for breakfast. Eight o'clock was the scheduled time for her nemesis, Barney Clark, to return to work and be reinstated. If he was a no-show, she could fire him and be done with it.

Though she hoped Barney wouldn't be on time, Emma feared he would. Yet she wouldn't squander the next hour in worry. She intended to enjoy breakfast with the priests and then hang out with Joshua and Chloe before school. Though she relished learning, school got in the way of her work for the Sovereign at the Temple—even though she could now complete all her lessons before lunch.

A yipping dog jolted her back to the present. Getting louder, Emma turned around as a puppy— one of those expensive designer breeds—bounded toward her. A smiling Barney trailed behind the unleashed animal. Barney never smiled. Something was up.

When Fred—her executive admin—had recommended they allow Barney to return as Emma's aide, she strongly objected. But realizing that keeping him close was the best way to keep him in check, Emma agreed. Fred intended that Emma would never have to be with Barney alone. She'd always have someone on her team present to ensure her safety. He had, after all, tried to kill her—in both the physical world and the spiritual realm.

But not expecting him until 8:00—if at all— Emma stood alone to face this evil man. *Sovereign*, she prayed silently, *give me strength and guide my words. Amen.*

Emma tapped her theatre training to mask what

she felt inside, intent on playing the role of a perturbed employer and not revealing herself as a trembling teenager.

"You're early." Emma narrowed her gaze to glare at Barney. "Your workday doesn't begin until 8:00."

"I wanted to make a good first impression as I embrace my new role here at the Temple. Please excuse my enthusiasm for wanting to make the most of it and prove to you how valuable I can be." Barney's dog bounced up to Emma and sniffed her feet.

Emma looked down. The dog's perky tail wagged with abandon. She needed to maintain her stern persona. "What is this?"

"It's a dog."

"Obviously, but why did you take it to work?"

"He's my emotional support dog. My therapist recommended a companion to help me properly deal with all I've been through . . . with all that *you* put me through, if I may respectfully add."

"I merely finished what you started." Emma cocked her head to the left and planted her right fist on her hip. She hoped it displayed her displeasure just as effectively as when her mom did it.

"Be that as it may," Barney said, "I sense you're not a dog person."

"I like dogs." Emma bent down to scratch the puppy's head. He rolled over so she could rub his belly. "I just don't like them at work."

"*It* is male, by the way. His name is Montgomery. He is Cavachon: part Cavalier King Charles Spaniel and part Bichon Frise."

"Sounds expensive."

"Nothing is too pricey to ensure my mental health."

Emma gazed at Barney's essence in the spiritual realm. He shone with his usual glossy black, which her mentor, Gabe, had said revealed the evil one's spirit residing within. Despite Barney's claims to embrace his new job, Emma confirmed that nothing had changed. He was still the same vile man and couldn't be trusted.

Yet she would now spend every day with him at her side.

## 2

_____

## RESCUED

"Oh, what an adorable puppy!" It sounded like Ashley. Emma turned around. It was.

Ashley squealed and dropped to her knee. She held out the back of her hand to the eager pooch. "You're such a cute little guy. Come here. Let me give you some lovin'."

The puppy bounded toward her, ears flopping and tail wagging. He sniffed her hand, and she scratched his head. His tail twitched with excitement. Ashley playfully caressed his head and ruffled the hair on his back. "I've always wanted a dog." He rolled over and whimpered for her to scratch his belly. He wiggled with glee over her attention.

"It looks like you found a new friend," Barney said. "His name is Montgomery."

Ashley's gaze darted toward the man. She recoiled. "What are you doing here?" She gave a worried glance toward Emma.

*Don't leave.* Emma mouthed to her new friend. *Please!*

Ashley stood and moved toward Emma and edged in front of her.

"I'm returning to work as the High Priestess's aide, starting today," Barney explained.

"I heard you might come back. But don't expect me to welcome you." At only a few years older than Emma, the cosmetologist's bold words surprised her. Emma welcomed having an ally at her side.

That's when Fred huffed up. "You're early, Barney!" The portly priest panted, catching his breath. "You're not supposed to be here until eight!"

"The High Priestess has already pointed that out, and I repent of my error. I apologize for my premature arrival. Rest assured that it won't happen again."

"I'll hold you to that." Fred stared at Barney. "Come with me, and we'll review the terms of your reinstatement."

"I also have some items I must cover with you." Barney planted his feet on the ground and glared at Fred.

Fred ignored him. "The key elements are that you're not to leave the High Priestess's side between 8 a.m. and 5 p.m., Monday through Friday. At all other times, you're confined to your quarters or must leave the campus. Understood?"

"Most assuredly."

"Follow me." Mark beckoned Barney. "There is paperwork to fill out and other details to review. Since you arrived early, we can get that done before you officially begin at eight."

The two men left Emma and Ashley, with Montgomery bouncing behind them.

"Thank you for not leaving me alone with him," Emma said. "You were so brave."

"Glad to help. I knew you were worried; you were as white as a sheet! Besides, Christopher told all the staff to make sure we never leave you alone with him."

"You're a good friend." Emma patted Ashley's back, which turned into a tight embrace.

"I'm headed to breakfast," Emma said. "Care to walk with me?"

As the pair turned toward the cafeteria, excitement gushed from Ashley's mouth. "Lunch yesterday with Topher turned out to be a date, just as I had hoped. It was bliss. Pure bliss. My little heart went pitter-patter." She patted her chest three times. "We spent the afternoon talking and went for a long walk. He held my hand." Ashley looked far away and sighed. "We're soulmates. I know it for sure. Thanks—again—for giving us permission to date."

"No problem," Emma said. "It was a stupid rule. Glad to help."

"Also, thanks for all the reforms you're making here. I'm so stoked about not being overworked and moving to a normal schedule. In fact, I now have extra time on my hands. This afternoon I'm going to help Beatrice—along with everyone else—get caught up on communications."

Before Emma could reply, Ashley continued her free-flowing monologue, something she excelled at. "I wonder what I'll do with my extra time once we get everything caught up. I was thinking, just maybe, I could offer cosmetology services to the staff here, too, and not just the priests. No charge. Kind of like an employee benefit? I did some calculations—not that I'm a math genius or anything—but I think it will work out just about right. What do you think? I think it'll be fine, even better than fine. Great, in fact. Don't you think so too?"

When Ashley drew another breath, Emma interjected. "It's a great idea! Why don't you talk to Christopher—and Frederick? If they agree, so do I."

Ashley stopped walking and gave Emma an enormous bear hug. "That'd be so cool! I'll be doing work I love and have time to spend with Topher when we're not working. Amazing! Couldn't be better." She gave Emma one last squeeze. "I'll start working out the details and let Christopher know." The pair dropped their embrace, and Ashley scooted off to her salon.

Emma went to the cafeteria, got her breakfast, and sat down with the priests. They had a lively discussion about what the Holy Text said regarding worship and Temple practices. The priests confirmed many of the insights Emma had gathered in recent months and recorded in her journal. One was singing portions of the weekly service.

Emma liked the idea. Before becoming High Priestess, she had landed the lead roles in many musicals. Yet she wondered how the people would receive her singing at services. She also wondered about the music, since the Holy Text only gave the words. Yet this was a challenge she was ready to embrace.

She gave the priests their blessing for the day and dashed off to school, hoping for some alone time with Joshua before their lessons began.

Emma burst into their latest meeting place—a hastily cleaned classroom in the old Temple school building. But her expectations for having some private time with her boyfriend evaporated.

**3**
_____

## CONFLICT

Joshua sat waiting for school to begin. Chloe was there too. Since they rode together each day, Emma should've expected this. But how could she have alone time with her new boyfriend and not disrespect her BFF in the process?

Chloe, however, proved her worth as the outstanding BFF that she was. She greeted Emma and then made a quick retreat, saying only that she'd be back when school started.

Emma rushed up and wrapped her arms around Joshua, giving him a ginormous hug. He responded with a quick kiss on her forehead. Suddenly Emma didn't care so much about school.

This was precisely the distraction their teacher, Jennifer, had warned them to avoid.

Facing Emma, Joshua held both of her hands and gazed into her eyes. "I have an idea," he said. "I think you're really going to like it."

Emma was sure she would. Thoughts of romance stirred in her heart. Her pulse raced. "What is it?" She looked up at him in expectation and gave him a coy wink.

"I know that you have most of your to-do list of projects here at the Temple done—"

"They're not done. Merely in progress."

Undaunted, Joshua pushed forward. "But the one thing that's pending is 'free the prisoners.' I have a plan."

"There's also 'restart the Temple school' and 'deal with the priests in Alpha group' for me to do."

"Yeah, there's that. But I want to help you free the prisoners, especially Mrs. Butler."

Emma's initial expectation for a romantic moment with Joshua faded, but freeing the prisoners—those wrongly accused of heresy and arrested for retraining —concerned her as well. It nearly happened to Joshua. Mrs. Butler, however, their former religion teacher back at Riverside High, was not so fortunate.

"Thanks to you, Captain Hernandez freed me only a few hours before my transfer to the detention center," Joshua said. "But the problem is we don't know where it's located, so we can hardly rescue the prisoners if we don't know where they are."

"At least Captain Hernandez learned there was only one retraining center and not several," Emma added. "But he guesses there could be as many as a thousand people there."

"I didn't know that."

"We need to free them." Emma scrunched up her face as she contemplated how she'd do this.

"I have the perfect solution." Joshua gleamed. "Captain Hernandez agrees. Since I was already arrested, put in the system, and scheduled for transfer, we just go ahead and do it. The captain will track where they take me. Then he can make a rescue plan to free the prisoners. It's quite simple, actually." With a pleased smirk, Joshua crossed his arms.

"No! Completely unacceptable." Emma crossed her arms too. "I won't allow it!"

"Why not? It's a great idea. I'm sure it will work."

"Too risky. We need to find another way."

Joshua pleaded, "Can't we at least discuss it?"

"No! End of discussion."

"Well, I'm going to do it." Joshua patted his chest. "Captain Hernandez agrees it's our best option."

"I won't allow it! As High Priestess, I command you to obey me and follow my wishes."

Joshua's shoulders sagged, and he looked at the floor. "You just played the High Priestess card on me." As his chest rose with resolve, so did his gaze. He glared disappointment. "You promised you'd never do that. You said that you being High Priestess would never affect our relationship."

"I'm just keeping you from making a huge mistake."

"Will you do this every time we disagree?" Joshua's eyes begged for Emma to relent.

She did not.

"Stop being stubborn," he hissed at her.

"Stop arguing with me. I've made my decision." Emma jabbed her pointer finger on his chest.

"If this is how you're going to treat me, then maybe this relationship isn't going to work out." Joshua turned his back to Emma and stomped out of the room.

Left in a stupor, Emma took the middle seat in the front row of the classroom. She fumed over what had just happened and Joshua's infuriating response to her concern for his safety. *Maybe we're not meant to be a couple after all. I think we're over.*

A few minutes later, Jennifer strode into the room and took her place at the front. Joshua trudged in behind her but sat in the back corner. Barney took the other corner. For her part, Chloe kept her distance from everyone. Tension filled the place. Emma set her jaw; her shoulders tightened.

Instead of focusing on her schoolwork, Emma let her anger take over. *I never wanted to be High Priestess in the first place.* She seethed. *Joshua doesn't respect me, and Chloe didn't stick around to support me. I'm done with them both! Plus, I don't want Barney messing with my life.*

As fury raged within Emma's mind and threatened to overtake her emotions, Jennifer pushed through the morning with dogged determination. It was the worst of all school days, and Emma couldn't wait for it to end. At only a few minutes before noon, Jennifer announced that their schoolwork was over for the day.

Joshua stormed from the room. Chloe stood, her eyes darting between Emma and Jennifer. Then she, too, left without saying a thing.

Emma lay her head on her desk, willing herself

not to cry over how badly Joshua had treated her and for Chloe's complete lack of support. *Who needs them anyway?*

Jennifer cleared her throat.

Emma sat up and stared at her.

"As your teacher and your friend, let me tell you this as gently and firmly as I can: You need to adjust your attitude and make things right with your friends."

Emma wanted to tell Jennifer exactly what she thought about this unsolicited advice, but the Sovereign told her to remain quiet. This was the first time she'd heard from the Sovereign all morning. Though Emma didn't want to obey, she did.

"Perhaps it might be best for you to consider what happened and what you must do to correct it." Then Jennifer left the room too.

*I don't need to do anything!* Emma fumed. *It's all their fault. I won't apologize.*

Emma wiped at her eyes when she heard footsteps plodding toward her. She didn't turn around to see who it was. She didn't care.

"Let's you and I take a walk." It was Gabe. The gentle words of her trusted mentor eased some of the tension from her rigid frame, but she didn't move.

He edged up to her and laid his gentle hand on her back. Its warmth comforted her. Peace flowed from it and eased into her body. Her shoulders relaxed and tension escaped her taut frame.

Emma relented to his tender suggestion and stood. That's when she noticed Barney squirming in the back corner of the room. *Great!* Since he was required to go everywhere she went, he had not only witnessed the rebellion of her two former best friends, but he'd also be there to witness what would certainly be Gabe's reprimand.

*Can my day get any worse?*

# 4

## GRACE

In silence, Emma and Gabe strode the Temple grounds. Twenty minutes later they wandered to the picturesque detention pond at the back of the campus. Without a word, they sat on a bench overlooking the grand vista. A large maple tree provided an idyllic canopy of shade.

The pond's ripple-free surface reflected the opposite shore's scenery. Smartly spaced ornamental trees dotted the perimeter of the pond, with an inviting walking trail circling everything. It was a most peaceful setting, but today Emma felt anything but peace.

She and Joshua had come here several times. It was *their* place. They'd sat on this very bench and taken in the beauty of the Sovereign's amazing creation. They'd held hands, shared their innermost feelings, and talked about their future.

*Joshua! What a turd. I was only trying to protect him, but he just wouldn't listen. Good riddance!*

Emma closed her eyes to shut out the serene surroundings. This way she could better wallow in self-pity. She willed her eyes to cry, to shed plaintive tears of suffering.

The Sovereign, however, wouldn't allow it, instead directing Emma's thoughts to her role in what had happened.

*I'm the victim.*

*No,* came the Sovereign's words implanted in her head. *You're the cause. Joshua's the victim. You're the turd, not him.*

Emma didn't want to hear this. She didn't want to consider that she caused their fight. She opened her eyes and glanced at Gabe. He sat next to her with the most tranquil look she'd ever seen. A smile played on his lips. He was at peace. She was not.

"You're right," Emma said to Gabe. "I need to accept responsibility and admit that I was wrong."

Gabe glanced at her in surprise. "I didn't say anything, but you have nonetheless come upon a most astute realization."

A gentle breeze caressed Emma's face. "I don't

know how this happened. How did things get so out of hand so quickly?"

"To put it in your vernacular, I believe the most insightful explanation is teenage hormones."

"What do you know about teenage hormones?" Emma corralled her hair and pulled it to the side, allowing the cool air to soothe the back of her sweaty neck.

"Though it resides far in my past—and may shock you to consider it—I, too, was once a teenager."

"Yet I shouldn't blame my behavior on hormones, should I?" Emma asked. "I need to control my emotions and not let them control me."

"Don't forget," Gabe said, "that you're a teenager striving to function as an adult, and in one of the most demanding of all positions. You're doing most admirably at it, I might add."

Emma cocked her head to the side. "Is that why I sometimes talk like a teenager and other times sound more like an adult?" Her stomach rumbled over having missed lunch.

Gabe ignored the noise. "Let me also remind you that most people here treat you as an adult, which surely adds to your confusion over what to say and what to do. Though it's a challenging equilibrium to navigate, you're doing an excellent job at balancing your teenage self with the adult role the Sovereign has placed you in. Do not allow discouragement to overcome you. Instead, press forward in faith."

Montgomery bounded up to the bench. His presence reminded Emma that Barney was lurking behind her and had likely heard everything she and Gabe had discussed. *How will he ever respect me if he knows what a mess I'm in?*

The small dog looked up at Emma. "Come here, boy." She slapped her thigh twice.

Tail a-wagging, he jumped onto the bench and snuggled on her lap. She scratched his head and then stroked his back. He lay his head on her thigh. Letting out a slow sigh, he closed his eyes.

"Just as the Sovereign offers you grace," Gabe said, "and you just offered it to Montgomery, you must also offer it to yourself and to Master Joshua."

"We use the word grace a lot, but sometimes I'm confused. What's it mean?"

"Considerate it akin to clemency."

"That's no help at all." Emma stopped petting Montgomery as she considered Gabe's words. Her stomach growled, startling Montgomery, who perked up and glanced her way. When she resumed stroking his back, he snuggled down again.

"Contemplate with care the implications."

Emma scrunched her left cheek as she thought about clemency. After a bit of deliberation, she offered her thoughts. "Does that mean grace is getting good things that we don't deserve?"

"Well stated."

"How can I offer Joshua grace? He's infuriating. Why am I so angry at him?"

"It's because you care for him," Gabe said. "You worry his plan could result in his harm and you'll be unable to protect him."

"Does that mean I'm right in wanting to keep him safe?"

"To the contrary. It means you must turn his future over to the Sovereign. Trust the Almighty to keep your boyfriend out of danger. Divine oversight is the best prescription in this case—as well as with most every other scenario."

"It's hard enough for me to trust the Sovereign with my future, let alone his."

"Placing our trust in the Divine comes with practice, perseverance, and maturity."

Emma let out a slow sigh. "I need all three." She exhaled slowly. "Like I said, it's hard."

"That's why it's essential for you to not be overly critical of yourself. Offer yourself a bit of grace over your struggles as you migrate from teenager to adult. Give yourself grace just as the Sovereign extends it to you."

Emma brought her free hand to her chin. She contemplated how to best put Gabe's wise advice into practice. That's when she remembered the time.

"Oh, no! I've got a meeting at 1:30. I know I missed lunch, but I can't be late for the meeting."

"Do not be alarmed, High Priestess," came Barney's words from just a few feet behind her. "I took the liberty of apprising Frederick of the situation. He canceled some of your meetings and attended to the others himself. This opened your afternoon."

Emma turned to him and scowled. "What did you tell him?" she snapped. "Did you say I had a complete meltdown and acted like a deranged banshee?"

"I merely informed him you were under a lot of stress and recommended you take the afternoon off. He agreed."

Given Barney's kind handling of the situation,

Emma felt bad for snapping at him. Yet, because of their combative history, she hesitated to apologize.

"Despite our past difficulties," Barney said, "know that I'm striving to turn over a new leaf, to treat you with the respect your high position deserves. I trust that one day you will also see fit to offer me grace."

Not ready to say "yes" or willing to say "no," Emma merely nodded.

"Also, please be aware it is now five o'clock and time for my workday to end."

"What!" She glanced at Gabe. "Seriously?"

Her mentor nodded.

"May you have a restful evening." Barney turned and snapped his fingers. "Come, Montgomery. Let us depart."

The tiny dog's head perked up and his tail wagged. He glanced at Emma and then jumped from her lap, racing to catch up with his owner.

As the two of them walked away, Emma turned to Gabe. "Though I wanted to blame Joshua for our fight, it's all on me. Thanks for being patient and setting me straight."

# 5

# RECONCILING

E mma arrived at the classroom in the old Temple school early the next day. She'd already apologized to Jennifer and now needed to patch things up with Chloe and Joshua. Her BFF was there but not her boyfriend. That was okay. She needed more time to process what happened and figure out what to say. He probably felt the same way.

With Chloe, however, they didn't need words— at least not many. With a whoop, they rushed toward each other and embraced, pulling each other into a tight hug.

Emma grew misty-eyed with emotion. "So sorry." It came out as a whisper.

"No problem," came Chloe's equally concise response.

They were good. Emma would deal with Joshua tomorrow. Today she needed to refocus on her studies and then her work at the Temple.

Emma and Chloe sat next to each other in the front row of the classroom and dove into their schoolwork. For his part, Barney had returned to his spot from yesterday in the back corner. Tucked under his arm was a new copy of the Holy Text. "I need something to read while you're studying, so that I don't go stark raving mad." He had said this with a shrug. Showing even passing interest in the Holy Text was the closest thing he'd ever said positive about their religion.

Emma and Chloe finished their schoolwork for the day, along with Emma redoing some assignments from yesterday she'd rushed through. That took them to lunchtime. After they ate, Chloe went to help Beatrice with communications. The focus was now on catching up the backlog of email messages.

Emma had a packed afternoon, covering Tuesday's regular schedule, along with a few meetings Frederick had postponed after her Monday meltdown.

Squeezed in the middle of it all was an appointment with the new Temple attorney, a partner at Marvin Miller and Associates. Emma and Fred walked into the large conference room in the palace. Barney trailed behind. Though he was expected to always be with Emma as her aid, his constant hovering provided a continuous source of irritation.

Emma's mom soon joined them, accompanied by the new attorney—who was also her coworker at her new job at Marvin Miller and Associates. Her mom introduced the attorney to Emma and Fred, while ignoring Barney, who stood rigid in the corner.

"I'd like you to meet my associate," Emma's mom said. "This is Lynn Robinson. Mr. Miller calls her 'the wizard of words' because her contracts are ironclad and she's skilled at finding flaws in other attorneys' work. We think she'll be an ideal match for what we need here at the Temple."

Lynn didn't look like what Emma expected, not at all. But Emma liked what she saw. Lynn looked younger than Emma's mom, so perhaps early thirties. She had a bright face and attentive eyes. Lynn wasn't wearing a high-powered, professional business suit. She wore a neat white oxford shirt and smartly tailored black pants. Instead of heels, she wore a stylish pair of flats. A simple, yet elegant, gold necklace adorned her neck, with earrings to match. She exuded confidence and competence. Emma liked Lynn's vibe. She was most approachable and would be an excellent fit at the Temple.

Emma looked at Lynn's spirit. It glowed. With a smile, Emma leaned forward and extended her hand. "Welcome to our team!"

Fred cleared his throat. "Actually, High Priestess, this meeting is to gauge suitability of fit, not confirming a new Temple resource."

"I can't tell if she's a good attorney," Emma said, "but I can certainly tell she's a good person and carries the Sovereign's favor. That's all I need to know."

Fred leaned back in his chair and stroked his chin. An amused smile formed on his lips. Then he relaxed. "I guess it's decided!" He leaned forward and extended his hand. "May I be the second to welcome you aboard."

Lynn took his hand and then turned to Emma and shook hers. "I understand my first task is reviewing your existing contracts to see which ones need to be overhauled and to ascertain any areas of oversight."

Fred nodded. "I'll get you started right away. Let me know what else you need or if you have any questions."

Emma interjected, "You probably know about the missing Temple money. My mom—I mean, Liz Barlow—uncovered that it went to priest bonuses. If a priest wants to return the money and not get in trouble, can you write a contract to make that happen?"

"Is there something I'm not aware of?" Fred asked.

Emma shook her head. "But I suspect we'll soon need it."

"I've learned to trust your instincts," Fred said. Then he turned to Lynn. "Given that, please make the drafting of this contract your top priority."

With that, all the adults stood. Uncertain, Emma followed their example. Everyone welcomed Lynn, including Barney.

As Lynn headed to the car, Emma's mom held back. Emma gave her a quick hug and asked about the sibs. "It's been days since I've seen them."

When her mom left, Emma rushed off to her next meeting.

It wasn't until after dinner at the cafeteria that Emma had a moment to herself. Instead of heading straight to her room in the priests' quarters, she took the long way, walking around the pond before looping back.

She thought about all that had happened today, both at school and at the Temple. She also wondered about Joshua. He wasn't replying to her text messages. She had tried a video chat after lunch, but he didn't answer. If he didn't show up at school, wouldn't respond to her texts, or answer her video calls, how in the world was she going to apologize?

Yes, she planned to apologize. Though it took her a day and then some to realize it, their fight was all her fault. She'd need to own up to it if she hoped to restore their relationship.

One priest huffed up in a partial jog, interrupting Emma's thoughts. It was Gavin, a priest from Beta group. "If I may," he said, "I have a personal query."

Emma stopped and smiled. She dropped her arms and let her hands dangle at her side. It felt awkward, but she wanted her body language to show she was approachable. "Sure! Shoot."

He paused and then launched into his question. "I understand you're investigating disappearing Temple funds and the bonuses some priests received. Hypothetically speaking, if a priest reluctantly accepted the bonuses and wanted to return the money, is there a way said priest could avoid prosecution, penalties, and prison time?"

"Our attorney is already working on that. How many priests are we talking about?"

Gavin didn't answer.

Now realizing his awkward choice of words to keep him from admitting guilt, Emma rephrased her question. "Hypothetically, how many priests are we talking about?"

"Seven," Gavin answered. "Everyone in Beta group. Hypothetically speaking, of course."

"I'll text Frederick, and we can meet to discuss this hypothetical situation."

"I appreciate your candor and your discretion."

Emma watched Gavin walk away, pleased with the idea of getting some of their money back. She didn't know how much it would be, but she already had several ideas of where she could spend it.

## 6

## THE PLAN

Joshua hadn't responded to Emma's attempts to reach him on Wednesday. When he didn't show up for school on Thursday, she grew concerned. The girls finished their schoolwork extra early and strolled the Temple grounds as they waited for lunchtime to roll around. Barney, of course, trailed behind Emma.

"I really like doing homeschool with you here at the Temple," Chloe said, "but I sure miss Lane. Could he maybe join us?"

"Lane!" Emma snorted. "I didn't think you even liked him."

"Oh, I do! I so do. He's real cute. And a smart

guy. Just thinking about him makes me tingle all over."

"Then why do you ignore him?"

"I guess I'm playing hard to get." Chloe fidgeted and then looked away. "But I don't know why. It makes no sense."

"You better let him know how you feel before he gives up and chases someone else. A lot of girls are interested."

"Having him in our little homeschool group would help me do just that."

"Jennifer already told me we couldn't add any more," Emma explained. "We're maxed out at three."

"I asked her yesterday, and she said it'd be fine. In fact, she said all your disciples can join us. What did she mean?"

Emma seethed that Chloe had bypassed her, but she corralled her frustration before she said something she shouldn't. "Jennifer's probably been talking to Gabe. From the very beginning, he's referred to our group as my disciples. I still don't get it."

"Now I do!" Chloe beamed. "It's a perfect description. We all look to you as our leader. Why not own it?"

Still angry, Emma glared at Chloe. "I'm disappointed you went behind my back."

Chloe drew away and cast an accusing eye at Emma. "I didn't go behind your back. I merely checked with her before I asked you. She's okay with it. What about you?"

"If she approved, it doesn't matter what I think, does it?" Emma pursed her lips and clamped her teeth.

"But it does. She said you have the final say. So what do you say?"

"You should've come to me first. As High Priestess, I oversee everything. At least I'm supposed to."

"It's not possible for you to know everything that's going on. That's why you have a team. Frederick is your executive admin, Mark is the chief of priests, and Christopher is your director of human resources. You picked good people. Let them do their jobs."

"And I'm her aid," wafted in Barney's words from behind them.

"Good point," Chloe said. "Plus, you said Jennifer would be headmaster when you reopen the Temple school. So why not let her lead now?"

Emma relaxed her posture and cast an appreciative gaze at her friend. "How'd you get to be so smart?"

"Which brings us to me and Joshua," Chloe said. "We're here to help you too. But it seems you keep shutting us out."

"I'm trying to do better," Emma said. "Please remind me next time I mess up."

"No problem."

Emma paused. "Speaking of Joshua, have you talked to him lately? He's been ignoring my texts and won't answer my video calls. I want to apologize for being a total turd to him on Monday, but how can I do that if I can't talk to him?"

Chloe stopped walking and looked up at Emma. "I thought you knew."

"Knew what?"

"He didn't tell you?"

"Spill," Emma said. "What's going on?"

"I thought you knew. He went undercover for Captain Hernandez to find out where the prisoners are being held for retraining."

Emma wanted to scream. She was angry; she was worried. She didn't know which emotion was stronger. But patience was the better answer. *Fill me with your peace, Sovereign*, she prayed silently.

The Sovereign did.

Instead of screaming, Emma held her roiling reactions in check. She forced out a long breath and inhaled just as slowly. "What do you know? Details. I need details."

Chloe looked up at her friend. "On Tuesday, he went to Captain Hernandez to finalize their plan. The captain returned him to his cell and reprocessed the paperwork for his transfer. It was approved yesterday, and this morning he was supposed to be moved to the detention center. The captain's been keeping me updated. I assumed he was updating you too."

"So it's too late to stop Joshua from his hair-brained idea?" Emma's eyes pleaded with Chloe to say that it wasn't.

Chloe didn't.

"Permit me to interject, Emma," Barney said. "My recollection is that you admitted your spat with Joshua was all your fault for trying to tell him what to do. Didn't you pledge to stop trying to control him?"

Emma suppressed the urge to snap at Barney. Though she didn't like him or trust him, he was correct. Emma hung her head. "You're right."

Chloe continued. "Their plan has all kinds of safeguards. Joshua has one tracker in his shirt and a different technology in his shoe. When they picked him up for transfer, one of Captain Hernandez's men attached a tracker to the van. Plus, they have a drone following the vehicle. It's a perfect plan and can't fail. We should know where the detention center is in a few hours, certainly by tonight."

"I just texted Captain Hernandez," Barney said, "to suggest he call you with an update."

Before Emma could thank him, her phone rang. She so seldom talked on the phone that it took her a moment to remember what to do.

Emma answered. Her eyes popped open, her jaw dropped, and her face blanched.

## 7

## MISSING

"What's wrong?" Chloe asked Emma in alarm as soon as she hung up the phone.

"They lost him!" Emma sputtered. "Captain Hernandez has no idea where Joshua is."

Chloe wrapped her arms around Emma and patted her back. "I'm so sorry. But I'm sure the Sovereign is with him and will keep him safe."

"Captain Hernandez was on his way here to update me in person when Barney texted," Emma added. "He says he'll be here in nine minutes."

"May I suggest, High Priestess, that we convene in the cafeteria and update your team," Barney said. "That way we'll all be on the same page. Then we can work together on the best way to proceed."

Emma went numb. All she could do was nod.

Barney texted Captain Hernandez to meet them in the cafeteria.

Emma spun around and began jogging. Panic surged through her body, and she broke into a sprint. Emma wasn't much of a runner, but she soon left Chloe and Barney wheezing in her wake. By the time she reached the cafeteria, emotions had overtaken her and flowed down her cheeks. Panting, she stumbled to her usual noontime table. There sat Jennifer, Fred, and Gabe.

"Joshua's missing!" she blurted. "Captain Hernandez is on his way here to update us."

Jennifer laid her hand on Emma's arm. "Emma, you need to breathe. You're about to hyperventilate. Catch your breath before you tell us what happened."

Emma gulped in air and spewed out the details. "Joshua went undercover to find where all the prisoners are being held for retraining." Her head spun and she grabbed the back of a chair as she sucked in another desperate breath. "He and Captain Hernandez had a plan, but something went wrong. The captain doesn't know where Joshua is. He's lost and alone!"

Emma broke down and fell into the chair.

"The Sovereign is with him," Fred said. "Joshua will be fine. Don't worry."

Emma lowered her head and rested it on the palms of her hands. Her shoulders quaked. Tears flowed freely. "The last time I saw him, we had a fight. It was all my fault. I yelled at him! What if I never see him again?"

Jennifer moved her hand to Emma's back. Someone else—Fred, she suspected—gave her a gentle pat on her shoulder. Their tender touches provided a bit of comfort but not enough. Emma lowered her head to the table, resting it on her forearm.

Emma stayed frozen in that position until she heard Captain Hernandez. "Emma, I'm here. Don't worry. We'll figure something out."

Emma straightened up. Mark, Christopher, and her dad—serving as doctor at the Temple clinic—were now there too. Her entire team was present. A tray of food sat before her. She knew she needed to eat to keep her strength up, but she sure didn't feel like it.

"Here's an overview," Captain Hernandez said to the group. "Joshua Hart volunteered to go undercover, posing as a prisoner, so we could determine the location of the retraining center. We had two trackers on him, as well as the vehicle they took him away in. We also had a drone surveilling them.

"Unfortunately, my agent didn't have time to properly attach the tracker to the vehicle, and it fell off soon after they left. They apparently found one tracker on Joshua while en route and threw it out the window. After about thirty minutes, the vehicle pulled into a warehouse. That's when the last tracker stopped transmitting.

"Six minutes later, four identical vehicles left the warehouse. The drone operator didn't know which one to shadow, but he dismissed the first one and the last one as too obvious. He followed the second one, but after twenty minutes, it returned to the warehouse. By that time, it was too late to track any of the other vehicles."

No one said a word.

In the lull, Captain Hernandez pulled out his phone. "I just received an update from my men that Joshua is not in the warehouse. It's reasonable to assume he left in one of the other three vehicles and is en route to the training center."

Emma stood. "Let's get moving."

"But we don't know where we're going," the captain said.

"I trust the Almighty will guide us," Emma replied. "The Sovereign often does that for me."

"While I appreciate your desire to react quickly," Captain Hernandez said, "our best course of action is to form a well-conceived plan and not charge off half-cocked. Besides, it's already getting too late in the day to set out. I recommend we prepare this afternoon and leave no later than 8 a.m. tomorrow morning."

Everyone but Emma agreed with the captain's recommendation, and they left. Gabe walked with Emma to her room in the priests' quarters.

"The Sovereign has assured me," Gabe said, "that Master Joshua is safe. You need to believe that as well."

"I reached out to him in the spiritual realm and could sense him, so I know he's alive. But something's wrong. I can't connect with him."

"I can't either," Gabe confirmed. "We must have faith."

## 8

## ROAD TRIP

Emma checked the time, the toe of her shoe tapping the dingy asphalt of the Temple parking lot. It was five minutes before eight. Captain Hernandez still hadn't shown up. She had obediently delayed searching for Joshua until this morning, even though she had yearned to leave last night. They were wasting time. The captain had said to wait. She was tired of waiting. He'd said they'd leave no later than eight. The minutes ticked by, moving to his deadline and then past it.

Emma willed herself to remain calm, despite her anxious emotions and agitated gut. She had to do something. Anything. *Sovereign*, she prayed silently, *still my racing heart and fill me with your peace. Be with Joshua and keep him safe.*

That's when the captain raced up, tires squealing as he rounded the corner. He was in a car, not the SWAT vehicle she'd expected. It was an aging clunker that filled Emma with doubt that it could survive a long trip.

Captain Hernandez jumped from the vehicle, slinging a beat-up backpack over his shoulder. He wasn't wearing his uniform, either, but was in street clothes. Something was up, and she feared it wasn't good.

He rushed up to her. "Sorry for making you wait. There have been some complications. I've had to shift our strategy accordingly. But I'm here now and will be ready to leave momentarily."

Not wanting to delay another second, Emma took a step toward his car, but Captain Hernandez held up his hand.

Emma stopped. "I'm confused." Emma studied his face for an explanation.

"I took the day off because our excursion is off the books. It's unofficial, which means we'll be forgoing the usual resources and support," the captain said.

"This is your plan? It took you all night to come up with this?"

"I indeed developed the most brilliant of strategies—if I may say so—but it was all in vain. Today we're going to have to plan as we go. I hope your deep connection with the Sovereign will help us move forward and achieve success."

That's when Topher—the former Temple chauffer turned accountant—pulled up in the Temple van.

"Here's our transportation." Captain Hernandez gestured toward the vehicle.

That's when Emma realized that Angie and Christopher had walked up behind her. Cocking her head to the side, Emma asked the pair, "What's happening?"

Angie spoke first. "I felt I needed to go with you today—just in case."

"In case of what?"

Angie shrugged. "I don't know, but I'm convinced this is where I need to be. Your father gave me his blessing and said he and Suzie would cover the clinic."

"I also felt an unexplained urge to accompany you," Christopher added.

Emma didn't know what to think of nurse

Angie's ominous explanation or Christopher's strange prompting. She hoped it was the Sovereign at work and would help bring success to their mission.

That's when Barney walked up, with Montgomery in tow. For once, the tiny pup was on a leash. He yelped when he saw Emma and tugged at his restraint to reach her. She bent down to ruffle his ears and scratch his head.

"This isn't necessary." Emma looked up at Barney. "I give you the day off."

"To the contrary," he replied. "My assignment is to be at your side, and that's exactly where I intend to be."

"We may not be back by five." Emma hoped to dissuade him.

"It matters not, for Montgomery and I have nothing pressing on our schedules this evening— nor for the entire weekend, for that matter."

This was not working out as Emma had expected. Instead of her and Captain Hernandez, it would be her, the captain, Topher, Angie, Christopher, and Barney, along with Montgomery. Instead of a highly provisioned SWAT vehicle, it would be an ill-provisioned Temple van. Instead of the backing of the police department and its vast resources, they were on their own.

Well, them and the Sovereign. But the Sovereign would be all they needed.

"Let's pray." Emma extended her hands to their group. "Lord, bless us today and guide what we do. May we have success for our mission and honor you. Oh, and keep Joshua safe. Let it be so." Emma lowered her arms and strode toward the van. Everyone followed.

Captain Hernandez rode shotgun, since this was his mission, and he was in charge—more or less. Emma and Angie took the middle seat, while Christopher, Barney, and Montgomery climbed onto the back bench.

"Lord, keep us safe as we travel," Emma prayed. "Direct us to Joshua and show us how to free the prisoners. Amen."

Everyone—aside from Barney, that is—chimed in with their agreement, giving Emma's prayer a heartfelt "Amen!"

"We'll head to the warehouse where we last had contact with Joshua," said Captain Hernandez. "Then we'll figure out the next step."

Emma glanced at her seatmate. She hadn't known Angie for long, but she'd liked the affable nurse from the start. Angie had proven herself as a capable healthcare worker and a devoted servant of the Sovereign. She also had the Divine Spirit within her, who had no doubt directed her to join today's ragtag mission.

"I'm curious, how long have you been supernaturally healing your patients?" Emma asked. "Did it cause problems at your last nursing job?"

Angie laughed. "It wasn't an issue, because I've only been doing it for the last two weeks!"

"Seriously? I assumed you'd been supernaturally healing patients for years."

"To be honest, I never even considered it as a possibility until the Sovereign used you to heal Christopher. Supernatural healing appeared long ago in the Holy Text, and you did it now, so I figured, why not try? I stepped forward in faith, and, through the Sovereign, healed many patients."

"When Dad told me about it, he assumed it was your normal practice."

"What else did he say?" Angie asked. "He seemed a bit miffed the patients were being healed before he could even see them."

"You're right," Emma said. "He didn't like what you were doing, but he also didn't like that it bothered him. I told him to let you do what you do best and for him to do what he does best. I think he accepted that."

Montgomery scooted up to Emma's feet. He jumped on her lap without being invited and looked up at her expectantly. When she ruffled his head, he rolled over and exposed his tummy. She hit just the right spot, and he quivered, with his tail thumping against her thigh in double time. He lay his head on her lap and closed his eyes.

Emma tipped her head back and closed hers too. She'd use this time to connect with the Sovereign and prepare her spirit. She needed to be ready for what lay ahead—whatever that might be.

# 9

# DIRECTION

When the van pulled off the road and stopped, Emma opened her eyes. They were at the warehouse. The captain instructed everyone to wait in the van while he investigated. Emma ignored him and followed him, hoping the Sovereign might reveal something to her as she looked about.

The Sovereign did not.

Captain Hernandez didn't spot any clues or have any insight into what to do next. Dejected, they slunk back to the van. That's when the Sovereign spoke to Emma. She relayed the instruction to Topher. "Take the next left."

He started the van and moved down the street.

At the next intersection, she said, "Straight ahead for two blocks."

Then came "right," followed by "veer left."

"It might be more efficient, Emma," Topher said, "if you just give me our destination."

"Unfortunately, I don't know where we're headed," Emma answered. "The Sovereign only gives me the next step when we need it. Though I can say that at this stop sign up ahead, take the road headed west and stay on it for two hours."

As they traveled, Emma reached out to Joshua spiritually. Though she could sense his presence, she couldn't connect with him or determine where he was. She only had a vague sense they were getting closer.

This confused Emma.

She and Gabe had often connected with each other in the spiritual realm. She and Joshua once did it too. Emma had tried it with both her father and mother, but those attempts fell short.

Though Emma best thought of this supernatural communication as telepathy, Gabe had informed her it was something much better. But she still didn't know how this connection worked. It felt like direct spiritual communication between two people. But maybe the Sovereign facilitated it. Or perhaps the Sovereign acted as a sort of supernatural conduit.

Regardless, Emma also knew that one party could keep the other from connecting. *Is Joshua blocking me? Why would he do such a thing?* Emma pondered these questions but came no closer to understanding how this special spiritual ability worked.

Two hours later, Topher stopped the vehicle at a T-intersection. "Left or right?"

Yet the Sovereign didn't reveal to Emma which turn to take. *Don't expect me to do for you what you can do for yourself,* the Sovereign whispered in Emma's mind. *You can figure out the rest on your own.*

"Not sure," Emma said. "Please pull off the road while I see which way to go."

Emma recalled the time when her spirit had left her body to ascend into heaven and commune with the Sovereign. Barney had found her nonresponsive body and rushed her shell to the hospital. But her spirit was intent on returning to her body in the exact place where it had left. Emma's untethered spirit bounced like a yo-yo between heaven and earth for quite some time. On one of her upward treks, the Sovereign taught Emma how to scan the horizon to locate her body. She did and found Joshua too. She wondered if that would work now.

After telling Angie what she planned to do, Emma closed her eyes and focused on the Sovereign, willing her spirit to rise. After a few seconds, her spirit disengaged from her body and went up. But only a few feet into her upward journey, it reversed course and reengaged with her body.

The Sovereign offered gentle correction. *Your spirit doesn't need elevation to scan the horizon. You can do it right from the van.*

Emma recalled what she had done before and tried to repeat it. With effort, and after a few false tries, she located Joshua. He was several hundred miles away.

She opened her eyes. "Turn left," she told Topher.

Emma continued to give directions to Topher at each intersection. Though she was taking them on the most direct route, it certainly wasn't the fastest. They traveled twisting country roads, which required slower speeds and extra caution.

Retrieving her phone, Emma pulled up a map. "There's a highway about five miles south that goes in the general direction of where we're headed. I think we'll make better time if we take it."

"An excellent suggestion," Topher said. "Aside from being painfully slow, these back roads are getting tedious. Plus, we'll need to refuel within the hour." Topher navigated to the highway and filled up the tank with gas. Next to the station was a quick serve restaurant, where they scarfed lunch to fill their rumbling stomachs. Not knowing when they'd eat again, they stocked up on snacks.

Captain Hernandez offered to drive, giving Topher a break. The former chauffeur readily agreed.

Soon they were speeding toward their destination.

For her part, Emma compared the direction she sensed in the spiritual realm with what she saw on the map. "In about two hundred and fifty miles, we'll need to get off the highway and return to back roads for the last bit."

About four hours later, Emma instructed Captain Hernandez to exit the highway. Topher resumed driving for the last leg of their journey. They had to backtrack a bit, but everyone agreed taking the highway was the best solution.

They were getting close. Not only could Emma

sense Joshua was nearby, but she also located Mrs. Butler's spirit. What a relief to know her former religion teacher was alive.

They drove through a tiny town. More correctly, it was a four-corner intersection in the middle of nowhere. Aside from some scattered houses, it offered a post office, aging motel, old-fashioned diner, and run-down convenience store and gas station. Down the road stood a large facility for the Lakeview County Consolidated School District. It was the only thing in the area that looked new.

"I think we'll find the detention center a couple miles down the road, just around the bend on the other side of that hill," Emma told Topher. "Let's pull the van off the road there and park behind the bushes. Then we can climb the hill to check things out."

Once again, Captain Hernandez wanted to go alone to scout the situation. Once again, Emma insisted she go along. He didn't even try to dissuade her. He retrieved binoculars from his backpack, and they worked their way up the hill.

What Emma saw shocked her. Given the claim that the prisoners were taken for retraining, Emma envisioned a school-like environment. What she saw, instead, was a prison compound. There was a singular rectangular building with no windows and one visible entrance. Surrounding it was a 20-foot chain-link fence with razor wire along the top. An armed guard staffed a single gated entrance. A watchtower with dual spotlights stood as sentry in the middle of the space.

Emma's hope for a simple resolution waned.

Captain Hernandez sighed. "This is going to be much harder than I expected."

## 10

# A FORMIDABLE CHALLENGE

It was dusk by the time Emma and Captain Hernandez made it back to the van. They filled in the rest of their group on the situation. Their collective optimism at being so close evaporated at what they faced to free the prisoners. It loomed as a formidable challenge.

At first, no one said a thing. Then everyone started offering their suggestions. All at once.

Not one idea made sense. They were all tired and hungry. Maybe food would help them think more clearly.

Emma looked at Hernandez. "Captain, what do you think about us heading to that little town we passed a few miles back to grab some food? And some rooms for the night?"

Everyone turned to Hernandez. "Don't call me Captain." He dropped his head. "I've been demoted to sergeant."

"Why?" Emma asked. "What happened?"

"When I complied with your request to release those being detained and awaiting transfer, that raised concern. This week they questioned the vast resources I've allocated to my investigations at the Temple."

"Investigations?" Emma asked. "Plural?"

"Four," Captain Hernandez replied. "First was the case where the four women refused to testify. Next is looking into who was behind the threats against you at school and the palace; I had planned to make an arrest next week. Third was investigating who tried to poison you. And I just opened a fourth case to investigate the missing funds at the Temple."

Emma gasped. "You've sure been busy!"

"They think I'm fixated on you. Now I'm the one under investigation."

"Does that mean we're on our own?" Emma asked.

"Not sure." Sergeant Hernandez shrugged. "I hope I still have enough pull to get them to dispatch a team to help us. But, frankly, I'm not sure."

Topher broke the silence that followed. "Let's get some food. Everyone buckle up."

When the van arrived at the diner, Emma hung back to talk with Sergeant Hernandez. "It doesn't feel right calling you 'Sergeant.' What's your first name?"

The former captain looked away, and then, with a sly smile, answered, "David. But I don't care for it. Most everyone calls me Hernandez."

"Hernandez it is. I'm sorry you got demoted and are under investigation because of me."

"I'm strangely at peace about it," he said. "You changed my life and gave me a purpose."

"The Sovereign changed your life," Emma corrected, "and will continue to do so."

"I hope you're not offended by me supposedly being fixated on you."

"I appreciate all you've done since I've become High Priestess. Thank you."

"I'm here to serve you." Hernandez gave a downward tip of his head to confirm it as fact.

"I didn't know you were ready to make an arrest. Who?"

"Barney Clark. Though Blane Abernathy committed the actual crimes, he said Barney's private security detail told him what to do. He implicated all four of them, but the one who physically attacked you was their leader. For their part, the four guards turned on Barney and agreed to testify he was the mastermind behind it all."

"Is the investigation dead?"

"I hope not. It's been turned over to my replacement for evaluation."

In silence, Emma and Hernandez strolled into the diner to join the rest of the group. Barney cast an odd glance their way. Something was up.

It was a quaint place. Already late in the evening, they were the only patrons there. They quickly ordered, and soon their food arrived. Yet, despite the much-needed nourishment to their bodies, their minds came no closer to figuring out what to do.

Perhaps a good night's rest would help.

They trudged next door to the motel, only to see a sign taped on the front door. It said, "Please see CJ at the diner." An arrow pointed in the direction they had just come. Making the quick trip back, they learned their waitress also doubled as the motel manager. They soon exited the diner with three room keys. One for Christopher and Topher. One for Emma and Angie. That left Hernandez and Barney—along with Montgomery—to share the third room.

Emma and Angie's room was dated but clean. That's what mattered.

Emma turned to Angie. "I was there when Joshua was first arrested. I think Hernandez was coming for me, but Joshua stepped in front of me, and they arrested him instead. That night, I couldn't stop thinking about him sitting in jail, along with all the other religious prisoners. I fantasized about what I could do to release them."

"Interesting," Angie said. "Tell me more."

"I'm not sure if it was my imagination or a supernatural dream, but I had three ideas that night. In one, I just walked up to the detention center and demanded everyone's release.

"Another one had me standing in front of the Senate giving testimony about the atrocities placed on these innocent people. There was media coverage. Public opinion swayed in my favor and soon forced the government to act.

"The third one was me raiding the detention center in the middle of the night. I wonder if that's what we'll be doing. Maybe that's why I subconsciously wore a black outfit."

"Since we don't seem to be making any progress

on our own," Angie said, "perhaps you should ask the Sovereign to reveal the next step to you tonight as you sleep. Has the Sovereign ever spoken to you in dreams?"

"A few times." Emma recalled her dream of finding sanctuary in the treehouse in Joshua's backyard. "It was both perplexing and amazing, but my dreams allow me to know exactly what to do when the time comes."

With that, they turned off the light.

Emma mentally reviewed the day, thanking the Sovereign for all the high points and trying to learn from the lows. Aside from Joshua's situation, the one thing she could've done better was thinking to take the highway sooner. But everything worked out, so it was all good. Emma ended by asking the Sovereign to reveal the next step as she slept. Soon she drifted off.

She dreamed she was back at the top of the hill, looking down at the prison compound. Suddenly, the whole place lit up like it was under a giant spotlight. "Now!" came the supernatural words booming from the heavens. Next, Emma found herself standing by the front gate, facing the guard. "I'm here to get the prisoners," she said. The guard got on his radio and simply said, "Release the detainees." Soon the captives streamed from the building and gathered in the prison courtyard. Emma turned and marched through the front gate. They all followed her out of the compound without any opposition.

Then Emma awoke. If only real life could be as easy as her dream.

## 11

---

## ACTION AT LAST

The next morning, the group checked out of the motel, scarfed a quick breakfast, and returned to the hilltop vantage overlooking the prison compound. Verifying that nothing had changed, Hernandez excused himself to make a phone call.

When he returned, his somber face told them everything they needed to know. "Despite my best efforts, I was unable to arrange for any support in freeing the prisoners. In fact, they placed me on probation and insisted I return immediately."

While the four men walked partway down the hill to discuss options, Emma stayed at the top. Angie glanced between Emma and the four retreating guys. She stayed with Emma, waiting in silence. Emma recalled the time she had cast evil out of the High Priest's residence in the palace. She had sanctified it and made it a safe place. She wondered if she could do the same thing for this large complex.

Emma peered into the spiritual realm to see what the supernatural conditions were at the prison. It was spiritually dark, pitch black. Junior demons flew about, shrieking with delight. From their place of safety inside the compound, they mocked Emma and her group. They taunted her to enter their lightless domain.

"Are you able to see into the spiritual realm?" Emma asked Angie.

The older woman nodded.

"Close your eyes and tell me what you see."

"It's completely dark and void of all good."

"Yes. What else?"

"There are hundreds of demons fluttering about. They think they're safe and that you can't harm them."

"They're wrong. Join me, and we'll cast them out."

"I don't know how to do that." Angie shuddered. "I'm afraid."

"With the Sovereign on our side, we have

nothing to fear." Emma reached out to hold Angie's hand. "Whatever you do, don't let go. There's safety in numbers."

They both closed their eyes. Their interconnected spirits flowed forward and breached the evil borders of the prison. Their auras shone brightly, pushing back the darkness and causing the demons to pull away. The evil spirits shrieked at Emma's bright, white light and Angie's soft blue glow.

"Don't you know the words of the Holy Text?" Emma mocked them. "It says, 'When danger surrounds you, the Sovereign will light your path, push back the darkness, and drive evil away.' May it be so here."

The demons trembled at those holy words. They screeched in horror as the truth assaulted them.

Emma and Angie's spirits moved further into the compound, their bright light shining further to push back evil.

"I command you, in the name of the Sovereign, to leave," Emma declared. "Be gone." With a flick of her ethereal wrist, Emma dismissed the evil minions. They skittered from her presence. "I forever ban you from this place and declare it a holy sanctuary under the jurisdiction of the Lord Almighty."

The demons recoiled, howling as they flew away from Emma's presence. In their haste to retreat, many collided, bouncing off one another. Yet they were soon gone.

Emma and Angie's spirits moved to the center of the compound, casting light in all directions. The darkness was gone. "I declare this a safe place forevermore," Emma pronounced. "No evil spirits or evil people may ever enter it again."

As Emma and Angie's spirits returned to their bodies, the spiritual reality at the prison compound continued to be illuminated by the Sovereign's pure light. The pair opened their eyes to a new reality, one not seen but nonetheless true.

Emma again reached out into the spiritual realm to search for Joshua. His presence was now stronger, as if no longer blocked by the forces of evil. She also located Mrs. Butler with ease, whom Emma sensed was standing next to Joshua.

That's when Emma's spirit connected with his. They could now exchange thoughts. She could hear what he heard and see what he saw.

"I'm not sure what just happened," Joshua said to Mrs. Butler. "But it's time. Now!"

The pair raced down a prison corridor, hastily unlocking prison doors with magnetic keycards as they slid by. Joshua opened the cells on his left, while Mrs. Butler did the ones on her right.

One by one, dazed prisoners emerged from their cells and followed their liberators in confusion. With about fifty prisoners freed, Joshua and Mrs. Butler turned to go down another corridor.

Rushing toward them ran two armed guards. Joshua and Mrs. Butler stopped, and the freed prisoners crashed in behind them. Planting their left feet, the guards angled their bodies and raised their guns. "Halt! Or die."

"Be careful, Joshua," Emma shrieked in her spirit.

That's when he blocked their connection, which stopped Emma from knowing what was happening. She tried to connect with Mrs. Butler but failed.

*Pop* came an ominous sound from inside the facility. *Pop. Pop.*

Angie gasped. "Is that gunfire?"

*Pop. Pop . . . pop.* And then a last *pop.*

All was quiet.

Emma reached out in the spiritual realm to find her boyfriend and teacher. She could sense them both, but something was wrong. Terribly wrong.

Their presence was no longer strong but barely discernible. They'd been hit. She was sure.

Emma knew what she must do. Turning to Angie, she said, "Wait here and pray I'll have the Sovereign's wisdom and power. Beg the Almighty for success."

With a nod, Angie closed her eyes. Her lips gyrated, and strange sounds whispered forth—just like Emma had heard from Gabe. Walking down the hill, Emma slid past the four men, still engaged in their fruitless discussions about what to do. Once back to the road, Emma followed its path to the main entrance of the prison compound. With her heart thumping inside, she exuded peace outside. Full of divine confidence, she strolled up to the gate.

The guard squared to face her but then relaxed when he recognized her. "High Priestess, we're honored by your presence." He kneeled and bowed before her.

"Stand up and join me. I'm here to receive the prisoners."

"I'm not surprised," he admitted. "A few minutes ago, something amazing happened. Something monumental. A strange peace flowed into this place, one that has never existed here before. Most of us felt it and knew something was about to happen. I now wonder why we're imprisoning these innocent people and what I'm even doing here."

"The Sovereign is at work," Emma stated.

"Yes, indeed!" The guard extended his hand to Emma. "By the way, High Priestess, my name is Jerry."

"Please call me Emma." She shook his hand. "Let us join with the Almighty to set the prisoners free."

Jerry picked up his radio and pressed the talk button. "I have exciting news! The High Priestess is here to receive the prisoners. Please open their cell doors. I repeat, open their cell doors."

Emma reached out and placed her hand on Jerry's military grade rifle. "You won't be needing this anymore."

"Yikes! It's getting hot. It's burning me." Jerry threw his weapon to the ground and gave it a kick, sending it skittering far away. Then he looked up and held up his hand, palm out. "Halt!"

Emma turned around to see Angie approaching the gate. "It's okay. She's with me."

"Good to know." Jerry beckoned Angie to join them.

Emma marched toward the doors of the ominous building, with Angie following on her right and Jerry on her left. The double doors of the prison burst opened. Two armed guards rushed out. They leveled their guns at Emma. "Leave immediately," the stocky one said, "or we'll shoot."

Angie screamed, and Jerry dropped to the ground. Emma didn't move. She stood strong. When they fired their weapons, she held out her hands as if to halt the bullets' advance. The rounds rushed forward but fell helplessly to the ground only a few feet in front of her.

Assured of the Sovereign's protection, Emma boldly stepped forward.

That's when a half a dozen more guards blasted through the prison's front doors. They rushed forward. But instead of charging Emma, they attacked the two guards and quickly subdued them, hauling them away.

Jerry stood and dusted himself off. "That should be the end of the opposition. I think everyone else is on our side."

Emma turned to the trembling Angie.

"That was intense!" the nurse said. "I had no idea I'd ever witness the Sovereign's amazing power like this, but now I have—just like we read in the Holy Text."

Prisoners began streaming from the building. Emma scanned the throng, searching for Joshua. She didn't see him. She also didn't see Mrs. Butler.

The rest of her team had now gathered behind her. She turned to Barney and barked out the first order she'd ever given him. "Go inside and make sure all the prisoners are free. Every one of them."

"Yes, High Priestess." He scurried off.

Then she turned to Christopher. "Please organize the people. Get Topher and Hernandez to help."

That left Angie. "You're with me," Emma said. "We must find Joshua before it's too late."

## 12

## FOUND

Emma sped toward the doors of the prison building, scanning the fleeing prisoners for Joshua and Mrs. Butler. *Please, Sovereign. Please.*

Emma didn't see them. Reaching the entrance, she paused.

*Trust me*, the Sovereign said.

Emma waited next to the doors. Joshua would need to go through them when he left. Hundreds passed by, but not Joshua. Her heart thumped. Her gut rumbled with worry. *Joshua!* She called out in her spirit, *Joshua, where are you?*

Nothing.

She didn't sense a thing.

With most of the prisoners out of the building,

the flow of freed people slowed to a trickle and then stopped. Panicked, Emma rushed inside. But she didn't know where to go. *Show me where to look*, she begged the Sovereign.

"Not to cause alarm, Emma," came Jerry's words from behind her, "but I understand some prisoners sustained gunshot wounds and were taken to the infirmary. We should look there first and hope for the best."

Jerry led the way. Emma followed, with Angie trailing behind.

The conscientious guard sped them down dimly lit halls and through unmarked doorways. "We don't have any medical staff here on the weekends, and the person on call has not yet arrived."

In no time, Jerry led them to the end of a shadowy hallway, pausing at a wooden door marked infirmary. He stopped while Emma pushed past. She opened the door and burst into the room. There lay Mrs. Butler on a gurney.

Her teacher turned to Emma in a daze. Her face bore bruises and cuts. More concerning, however, was her blood-soaked top, with her shoulder area having the deepest concentration of red. Though less pronounced, the lower part of her right pant leg revealed the sign of more trauma.

"Emma!" Mrs. Butler stretched out her hand. "I sensed you were nearby."

Emma reached out to hold her teacher's hand. It was clammy. Emma laid her other hand on Mrs. Butler's forehead. "Sovereign Lord, by your Almighty power, I declare complete healing for Mrs. Butler. Take away her pain and restore her to full health."

Mrs. Butler inhaled slowly, a relieved smile forming on her lips. "I'm already feeling better." A tear seeped from her eye.

Emma looked at her teacher's bloody shoulder. She moved her hand to hover over where she sensed the bullet had entered. The Sovereign told her what to do next.

Emma looked at Mrs. Butler. "I'm afraid this might hurt, but we need to get the bullet out."

"Do what you must do. I trust how the Sovereign is leading you to bring about my healing."

With care, Emma rested her hand on Mrs. Butler's shoulder. Emma closed her eyes and filled her lungs with air—and her being with divine courage. "I declare that this bullet has no place in this body. I command it to loose itself and come out."

Mrs. Butler gritted her teeth and grimaced. She clamped her eyes shut; tears leaked out.

Emma felt movement underneath her hand. Soon something poked it. A few seconds later, the bullet popped out of Mrs. Butler's shoulder and deposited itself into Emma's waiting palm. Still, it surprised her. Emma pulled her hand back, turned it over, and loosened her fingers. She gasped at the presence of a bloody slug lying in her hand. She flung the still-hot bullet into a nearby wastebasket. It landed with a metallic thud.

"That was amazing," Mrs. Butler said. "Yes, it hurt as it came out. It hurt a lot. But I feel better already. Will you do the same thing with the one in my calf?"

Emma moved her hand to Mrs. Butler's pant leg, above where she sensed the bullet was lodged. Again, she gently rested her hand on the wound and commanded the projectile to come out. It did. She tossed the bloody slug into the trashcan.

Frozen in amazement, Angie had watched everything Emma did. Now Angie shifted into nurse mode, rapidly assessing her patient's condition. Jerry pulled an assortment of supplies from various cabinets in the infirmary. "We don't have much to work with, but I think these will help."

As Angie attended to her patient, color returned to Mrs. Butler's face. It was clear she would be okay. That's when Emma made her urgent inquiry as gently as possible. "Mrs. Butler, do you know where Joshua is? I'm really worried."

Mrs. Butler glanced away, but her eyes soon returned to peer into Emma's. "I'm so sorry."

"What? Tell me!"

"He's on the gurney behind you. He didn't make it."

## 13

### LOST

Emma turned. Pushed into the corner was another gurney, a sheet draped over it. She rushed forward and ripped back the cover. It revealed a body bag. Emma's heart about burst in her chest. With trembling fingers, she reached out and slowly unzipped the bag. She gasped at the confirmation of what she feared. There lay Joshua's inert body.

His face looked like what Mrs. Butler's had, only worse. Far worse. His tattered shirt, also drenched in blood, revealed the entry point of two bullets into his chest and a third into his bicep.

Emma caressed his cheek. It lacked warmth. Lifeless. He was dead. She knew it, but her eyes begged Angie to come over.

The nurse did and soon confirmed Joshua had passed. She wrapped her arms around Emma. "I'm so sorry," she said while offering comforting pats. "I'm so sorry."

After several seconds, the pair released their grasp of each other. Without a word, Angie returned to attend to Mrs. Butler. Emma turned to stare at Joshua.

"No!" She dropped to her knees and sobbed, clutching at Joshua's arm. *Sovereign*, she complained silently. *You told me to trust you. What happened? Did I do something wrong?*

Yet Emma knew this wasn't her fault. It wasn't the Sovereign's fault either. It was the fault of evil. It was that simple. Evil killed her beloved Joshua. The future they'd planned—and the Sovereign had promised—would never happen. Their dream of life together was gone, snuffed out with a bullet. *If only you would've listened to me.*

Emma lowered her head to rest on Joshua's arm. She no longer cared she was the High Priestess. She forgot about the thousand prisoners she had helped free. All she wanted to do was scream. She didn't want to study anymore, lead worship again, or be the Sovereign's agent of change. She just wanted Joshua, but that was not to be.

On impulse, she placed her hand over the wound in Joshua's bicep. An inner compulsion told her to remove the bullet. "Come out," she declared, although in a soft whisper, hesitant and full of doubt. His arm twitched. The bullet moved. Soon she held the projectile in her hand.

Moving to his chest, Emma repeated the process over the smaller of the two wounds. This time she spoke with more confidence. The bullet obeyed her command. The third bullet took longer to emerge, but it also complied.

She cast all three aside into the trash.

Filled with a tinge of hope, she studied Joshua's face. Yet nothing changed. She looked at his chest, willing it to rise and suck in oxygen. It didn't. What little hope that remained quickly disappeared.

She stayed frozen in the moment, numb to all that was happening around her. Behind her, someone burst into the room. She didn't care who.

"I can confirm that all the prisoners have been released." It was Barney. "If you want . . . Oh, no!"

Emma heard his feet shuffle toward her. "My dearest Emma, I'm so sorry." Barney rested a gentle hand on her shoulder.

She spun around and screamed. "Get your dirty paws off me! I told you to never touch me again!"

Barney took a step back and held up his hands to signal regret. "My apologies. I didn't intend to defy your past wishes and merely wanted to offer comfort. I, too, have suffered significant loss and am here to offer whatever support I can."

His gentle words and sincere tone made Emma regret her overreaction to his attempt to console her. "Sorry." Given the situation and all the baggage of their past, it was all Emma could offer.

Barney kneeled next to her. "I know that all you want to do right now is sit in your grief. That's understandable. I get it. But you also have a thousand people looking to you to lead them out of this mess. A wise leader puts the needs of their followers ahead of their own. I encourage you to focus on them and mourn later. Know that I'll do whatever I can to help. Just tell me what you want me to do."

Still kneeling, Emma pivoted to look at Angie. The kind nurse nodded her agreement. "I'm afraid he's right."

"I won't leave his side!" Emma said. "It doesn't make any difference, but I will not abandon him."

"I pledge to keep vigil in your stead," Barney said, "and promise not to leave him until you make arrangements. I'll also stay here and watch Mrs. Butler on your behalf."

Emma stood and wiped the tears from her face. Jerry handed her a towel, which she gladly accepted and used to clean herself up as much as possible.

As Emma prepared herself to leave and lead the people, Angie readied herself too.

"Mrs. Butler is in stable condition and only needs rest. I feel I'm more needed elsewhere." Then Angie looked at Barney. "Text me if you have any questions or concerns."

Emma turned to leave, suppressing an irrational urge to hug Barney. For the first time since she'd known him, he'd truly done something in her best interest. Yet she couldn't push aside the fact that only a few weeks ago he had tried to kill her—twice. As Fred had advised, "Keep your friends close and your enemies closer."

*But is Barney still my enemy?*

## 14

### WE MUST LEAVE

As Emma left the infirmary, she prayed silently. *Lord, give me your strength to cover my weakness. Guide me in what to do. I so need you, now more than ever.*

*You can count on me,* came the Sovereign's response. *Trust me.*

But given that Joshua was dead, Emma really wondered if she could trust the Sovereign. Yet she knew that trust was her best option—perhaps her only one. *Sovereign, take what little faith I have and replace my doubt with your grace.*

Jerry guided Emma and Angie to the building's main exit. They moved outside. Emma trudged forward to rejoin her team.

As she did, the Sovereign's next instruction came. *You must lead the people away from this place.*

Her team—her friends—received her as she walked up. No one asked about Joshua. She was glad. She didn't know what she would say or if she could even answer without crying. Tears would need to wait until everyone was safely on their way home.

Emma looked at Christopher. This was all the encouragement he needed. "We've had the people group themselves by district. Hernandez went around and appointed a leader for each group. Topher did his best to answer questions and address concerns."

"Well done," Emma said.

"Now we just have to figure out the next step," Christopher added.

"We must leave," Emma said. "As soon as possible."

Christopher cast a questioning glance her way. "I think we're better off to remain here until we can arrange for transport."

"I agree with Emma," Hernandez said. "If we stay here, we're sitting ducks. As soon as the next shift of guards arrives, they can easily re-imprison everyone. But once we leave the premise, they can't touch us."

"Why's that?" Christopher asked.

"Because their staff released the prisoners," Hernandez said. "Since the prisoners didn't escape, and we didn't take them by force, there's nothing the guards can do to take them back once we leave the facility. But we must leave."

"Let's get everyone out of here," Emma said. "Then we can figure out how to get them home."

"I'll get a bullhorn," Jerry said. "That will make it easier for you to communicate with everyone."

As he scurried away, Emma's phone vibrated. It was a text from Chloe.

"Heard the great news from Hernandez that you released the prisoners," the message read. "Lane and I came in today to work on the backlog of email, but we're available if you need us."

"Maybe you could post updates on the website," Emma texted back.

"We already talked about that. Beatrice is great at communications, but tech isn't her thing. It's Lane's. I'll get him working on it right away. Just tell us what you want posted."

That's when Jerry rushed up with a bullhorn.

He handed it to Emma, who passed it off to Christopher. He shrugged and gave it back to her.

*Sovereign*, she prayed, *give me the right words to say to lead your people to safety.*

Then Emma looked around. "Though they'll be able to hear me, they won't be able to see me."

Hernandez dropped to his knees. "Stand on my back."

"Seriously?"

"Yes. It's no big deal." He leaned forward and placed his hands on the ground.

Emma kicked off her shoes. With hesitation, she climbed on his back, standing on his shoulders. Christopher and Topher stood on each side to steady her.

She pressed the talk button and brought the bullhorn to her mouth. "Attention everyone. Attention. It's important that we leave the prison grounds as soon as possible. There's a school a couple miles up the road. We'll head there. Go by district. Once we're safely away, then we can work on getting everyone home.

"We also want to let your families and friends know that you're here and all right. As you leave, we'll take a video and post it online. If you don't want to be on the video, just turn away from the camera."

Emma lowered the bullhorn but then brought it back to her mouth. "One more thing. Since everyone walks at a different pace, don't worry about staying with your group. Your group's leader will go first. Appoint two people to follow the rear. We don't want anyone left behind. Once we get to school, you can reassemble into your districts. Thank you."

Aided by Topher's steady hand, Emma stepped off Hernandez's back, who seemed unaffected by filling in as her platform.

"Christopher, will you go with the first group and help organize everyone in the school parking lot as they arrive? Topher and Hernandez, will you video the people as they leave? Do one group and then send the video to Chloe and Lane. They'll put it up and link it from our website. Switch off with every other group." They all nodded.

"Angie, will you see if anyone needs immediate medical attention or might not be able to make the trip?"

Jerry stepped forward. "What would you like me to do?"

"Thanks for volunteering," Emma winked at

the guard. "Will you stage the groups and send them out in an orderly manner? Make sure there are two people following each group."

"I appreciate you trusting me to help. I so want to make amends for my role in being part of this injustice."

As Jerry headed off, Emma surveyed all the people, wondering what she had overlooked. That's when she noticed Angie, giving her an imperative wave. She jogged over to the concerned nurse.

"We have two people who sustained minor gunshot wounds," Angie said. "Will you remove their bullets?"

Emma looked at a young woman standing behind the nurse.

"Though it hurts a lot, I think I'm okay." Yet the woman's face told a different story. She glanced at her forearm.

"I'm afraid this is going to hurt," Emma said, "but the pain won't last long."

The woman nodded.

Emma placed her hand over the woman's forearm and commanded the bullet to come out. It did. Emma didn't know what to do with it, so she shoved it into her pocket. "Sovereign, Lord, remove this woman's pain and make her whole again. So be it."

"That's amazing! I can hardly believe it. Thank you so much!" The woman turned away but then glanced back at Emma. "May I keep the bullet? A souvenir?"

Emma pulled the still-bloody bullet from her pocket and dropped it into the woman's cupped hands. "May it always remind you of what the Sovereign did for you today."

A middle-aged man stood next in line. He'd been hit in his upper arm. Clutching his elbow, he pulled his arm tight to his torso, bracing for what would happen next.

Emma commanded the bullet to leave, and it did. "Would you like a memento?" She gave him the bullet and then proclaimed complete healing over his body as well.

Emma turned to Angie. "I think we heard seven shots."

Angie nodded. "There were two bullets in Mrs. Butler, two in these individuals, and three in Joshua. I think that means we're done with bullets for now, hopefully forever."

Hearing Joshua's name reminded Emma that he was gone. *How can I ever hope to do this without him?*

## 15

### AWAY

Emma tried to push aside her pain over Joshua's death. She prayed to the Sovereign for the strength to do what she must do.

Emma breathed deeply several times to regain her composure. Once ready, she pulled out her phone to record a social media post.

"Hi! Emma Barlow here. I have exciting news! I'm pleased to announce that everyone falsely arrested for heresy and sent for retraining has been released." She pivoted her phone away from herself and panned the prison compound, pausing on the people marching out the front gate.

Turning the camera back to herself, she continued. "Once we're safely away, we'll work on a plan to get everyone home. Look for updates on the Temple website. As we speak, my friends are adding a new page to give the latest info. We'll add a link to this post as soon as it's ready. Thank you for all your support during this ordeal. We're glad it's almost over and everyone will soon be home." Emma paused and then added a needed postscript. "Please join me in praising the Sovereign for making this happen." Emma pressed stop on her phone.

As she posted the video on social media, Angie strode up, along with two older women she felt might not be up for a two-mile trek. "Perhaps they can ride in the van?" she said.

That seemed like a good idea, yet the van wasn't there. When Topher finished videoing the second to the last group, Emma sent him to retrieve the van. Then she texted Barney for an update. It wasn't long before he and Mrs. Butler exited the building, maneuvering the gurney that carried Joshua's body. Emma nearly retched at the sight of the body bag that held his shell.

She was still trembling as Barney walked up. "Be strong, Emma. You can do this. I have confidence in you."

Emma's head subtly bobbed in agreement as

she received his words. "Thank you for staying with him . . . and for encouraging me."

That's when Topher returned with the van.

Emma turned to Mrs. Butler, who looked fine and showed no hint she'd been injured. "I'm glad to see you're up and about, but to be safe, maybe you should ride back in the van."

As Mrs. Butler climbed into the passenger seat, Barney and Angie placed Joshua's body bag in the storage compartment of the van. As they opened the rear doors, Montgomery bounced out. He spotted Emma and ran up to her with a yelp, ignoring his owner. Emma glared at Barney and then Topher. "Please tell me he wasn't locked inside the van this whole time."

"No worries," Topher said. "Montgomery was safely secured on his leash outside the van and under shade. He had plenty of water. He was quite fine the whole time, just a bit lonely."

After giving Montgomery a quick scratch on his bobbing head, Emma opened the side door of the van and helped the two older women climb in. Angie slid next to them in the middle seat. Barney moved to the third row, which meant Emma would need to sit next to him. But for the first time since she'd known him, she wasn't concerned.

Before Emma climbed in, she glanced around the compound. All the released prisoners had left. Only some of the staff remained. She looked at Jerry, grateful for what a big help he had been. "I wish you could go with us, but I'd like you to stay here and keep us updated."

"I was hoping I could go with you too," Jerry said. "But you're right. I can best help you by staying here, for now. One day I hope we can reconnect. I'd like to become a priest, if such a thing is possible."

"I hope to reopen our Temple school to train future priests," Emma said. "We're not ready to do that yet, because we have no place to house them. But when we do, let me know if you're still interested, and I'll make sure you're one of the first to be invited."

"I'll be counting the days," Jerry said. "Be safe."

"You, too, my friend." With that, Emma got in the van and pulled the door shut. Though she wanted to walk with the rest of the former prisoners, she knew she had to get to the school as soon as possible to plan the next steps with her team.

They drove slowly past the progression of people, waving their support and giving encouragement.

"Topher!" Angie yelled. "Stop the van. Someone needs help."

She jumped out before Topher could even stop and ran up to a middle-aged man. His face was blotchy. He wobbled as he struggled to breathe.

She guided him to the van. Emma opened the doors and climbed out. She and Angie helped the man climb in. He moved to the backseat with Barney, and Angie slid in next to him. Emma sat next to the two older women in the middle seat.

She hoped they wouldn't need to pick up anyone else, because they were about out of room.

As the van moved forward, they soon passed Hernandez, jogging down the road at a brisk pace. He wouldn't be far behind them.

## 16

## PROVISIONS

The van pulled into the school parking lot, where about two hundred people had already gathered. The rest were still en route.

Even though Joshua was in a body bag, Angie suggested Topher park under a shade tree to keep his body out of the hot sun.

As Angie attended to her three patients, Emma and Barney walked over to where Christopher stood. Soon Topher joined them. Hernandez arrived shortly thereafter, breathing hard but not spent.

Then Angie joined them. "The man we picked up is okay, but he needs water. We all do. Our next pressing need is food. Everyone ate breakfast at the prison, but it'll be lunch before we know it. We have nothing to feed all these people."

Emma nodded to confirm she heard, but she didn't know what to do. "Almighty Lord," she prayed aloud, "will you show us what to do and give us supernatural insight? Grant us favor with those who can help us. Amen."

Emma surveyed the group as they each opened their eyes and looked at her. "I think flying is the quickest way to get people home, but I'm not sure where the airport is or how to get everyone there."

"I recommend buses as our best option," Christopher said. "I have a contact at a charter bus company. He's the VP of operations, and I put in a call to him. I hope to hear from him shortly."

"My thought was trains," Topher added. "But we have the same issue of getting to the train station—wherever it is."

"Another concern is us being here at the school," Christopher added. "Though it's a public facility, and we have every right to be here when school's not in session, I think someone in authority should know about it."

Emma perked up. "CJ, the waitress at the diner, said she'd lived here her whole life. I bet she knows who we should contact."

"I'm on it." Angie pulled out her phone and stepped away from the group.

"I'm getting great coverage on my social media posts," Emma said. "Some have even gone viral. But I think media coverage will help us reach more people. They can tell the entire country about our situation."

Barney spoke up. "I have contacts at all the major networks. Let me make a few calls." He, too, pulled out his phone and walked away.

Emma returned her thoughts to Angie's pressing need for water. She turned to Topher. "Will you go back to the convenience store, and buy all the water they have?"

"Consider it done." Topher jogged back to the van and drove away.

"Let me make another call to the bus company," Christopher said.

That left Hernandez. He looked at Emma, waiting for her to tell him what to do. Yet at the moment, there was nothing.

That's when four vans bearing the prison's name pulled into the school parking lot.

Emma gasped. "Do you think they're coming to take the prisoners back?"

Hernandez unshouldered his backpack. His

hand dove inside and retrieved a pistol. "Not if I have anything to say about it."

Emma held out her hand. "Put it back. Let's look for a peaceful solution. Besides, I doubt your one gun would make much difference if they all have rifles."

The vans stopped. A beaming Jerry jumped out of the first one. "We have food! It'll just go to waste since we no longer have any prisoners to feed. You might as well have it."

"Brilliant!" Emma turned to Hernandez. "Will you organize the people so we don't have a stampede?"

"I brought my bullhorn." Jerry grinned.

With military precision, Hernandez instructed the people how they would proceed and what the consequences would be if they disobeyed. After his initial instructions, Hernandez only needed to use the bullhorn two more times to correct a few impatient people. But they quickly got back in line at his stern reprimand.

As Hernandez oversaw the food distribution, a smiling Angie returned. "That was a piece of cake. CJ knew exactly who we should call. The principal is her daughter! She only lives five minutes away and will be here soon."

That's when Topher returned with a van full of bottled water. It was a lot, but they'd have to ration it to make sure they didn't run out.

"Count how many bottles you have," Emma said. "Then plan what to do."

She'd barely finished speaking when a minivan drove up. Out came a younger version of their waitress. Casually dressed, she strode up to Emma with confidence. "I'm Carli, High Priestess. I understand you've already met my mother."

"You look just like her." Emma extended her hand.

"We often hear that." The principal scanned the parking lot. "Looks like you have about a thousand people here, give or take. I see you have food and water. I can provide shelter and restrooms inside the school. Though you can use the cafeteria to eat in, I can't provide any food. We only have enough on site to feed our students on Monday. Their needs are my number one priority."

"I agree," Emma said. "We appreciate any help you can give us, but the students come first."

"I'll open the building."

Emma thanked the Sovereign for all these provisions and the speed at which they arrived. She barely finished her prayer of thanksgiving when

Barney returned. "The media is on their way. But it will take the closest crew a couple of hours to arrive."

A pleased Christopher returned to share his update. "The charter bus company is eager to help in any way they can. My contact will also reach out to his counterparts at ABT airlines and the rail company."

"Maybe they'll have some ideas about how we can get people to the airport and train stations."

Emma paused, her mind spinning from the flurry of answered prayer and the rapid speed at which help arrived. "I think it's time for me to post another update."

She pulled out her phone and pressed record. "Emma Barlow here with exciting news. I and all the released prisoners are away from the prison. Everyone is safe, well fed, and cared for. We're now planning on how to get everyone home and will post updates on our website."

Emma stopped the video and posted the recording.

Thanks to Hernandez's organization—and his commanding expectation that everyone would comply—the people had all eaten without incident. Some remained in the parking lot, but most had gone inside. They wanted to get out from under the sun or use the restrooms.

Emma walked over to Jerry to thank him. He dismissed her appreciation with a humble shake of his head. "I'm happy to help. It was the right thing to do."

Emma thanked him again.

"Our plan is to return late afternoon with enough food to feed everyone," Jerry said. "But shift change will happen at six, so you might not receive any more meals after that. I'm also not sure what their reaction will be to your departure. Some will be supportive, and others could be hostile. I'll keep you updated."

## 17

### TIME TO GRIEVE?

Emma had a few minutes to herself and wondered if she had time to grieve. Yet she didn't know how. She'd never lost someone close to her. Screaming and bawling might offer a bit of relief, but was that the best way for her to mourn and move forward?

*I so wish Mom was here.*

Emma longed for someone to hold her hand and tell her everything would be all right—even though it wasn't. Emma recalled when she was little and scraped her knee or cried over the words of a friend. Mom always knew what to do and said the right things.

*But Mom isn't here.*

The whirling blades of a helicopter moving

toward them ended her thoughts about grieving. She turned to Hernandez. "Should we be worried?"

"Friendlies," he said.

"Friendlies?" Emma asked.

"It's a civilian copter, not military or law-enforcement, so we can expect the occupants will have friendly intents."

The helicopter set down on a nearby hill, safely away from the school and all the people. When it was okay to approach, Christopher walked up to greet the occupants as they emerged from the cabin.

Emma jogged over to meet them and confirm they were "friendlies."

It was a representative from ABT airlines, whom Christopher's contact at the charter bus company had reached out to. She was there with a team of two to coordinate logistics. They set up shop under the overhang at the school's entrance. They each had a laptop and a lot of communication gear.

"Providing local transportation is our first concern," the team's leader said. "As I work on that, my team will figure out the most effective way of getting everyone home as quickly as possible. We'll use planes, trains, and buses. But first we need to know how many people we're talking about for each district."

Hovering in the background, Topher stepped forward. "I have numbers for you, and we're working on getting a list of names." He pulled out his phone and showed her the screen. She tapped one of her associates to jot down the numbers.

Carli also had overheard the exchange. "If it will help, we can use school buses to get people to the airport and train stations. Since most of our students arrive by bus, we have more than enough, but they must be back by Sunday evening so it doesn't interfere with school on Monday. If you agree, I can contact our head of transportation to alert our drivers."

"Please do," came the leader's reply.

An hour later, Topher returned with a list of all the people who needed to go home, organized by district.

Grateful for this information, the team leader shared her plan. "Based on the numbers from each district, we'll send home three districts by train, eleven by plane, and the rest by bus. We'll have schedules for you shortly."

Topher also had a second version of the list for Chloe and Lane to post online. Most people readily

gave their full names, but some used initials or nick-
names to protect their privacy, while still letting
their loved ones know they were safe and on their
way home.

Emma turned to Christopher. "Once you know
the schedules, please send them to Chloe so Lane
can post them online. That way, their families will
know when to expect them."

With everything falling into place, Emma again
pulled herself away, wondering if she could focus
on herself for a moment and deal with her pain—
before she exploded.

Yet alone time was not to be.

## 18

## INTERVIEWED

A team from the network sped into the parking lot. The crew jumped out and began hasty preparations for a broadcast.

A pleased Barney strode up to review his expectations.

Once everything was ready, a reporter marched toward Emma with head held high. She was mid-twenties and had straight black hair that danced on her shoulders each time she moved her head. With trendy attire and wearing more makeup than Emma thought was wise, Emma didn't trust her. The woman swooped in. With a fake smile, she glinted at Emma. "Are you ready for our interview?"

"Interview? You should talk to Barney Clark. He set this up."

"But he promised us an interview with the High Priestess. We paid for an exclusive."

Emma didn't know what this meant, but she assumed it meant she'd have to do an interview. She'd done a few small ones in the past; they didn't bother her. But with sorrow over Joshua's death simmering in her mind, she didn't feel like talking.

"Take a deep breath. We go in three." The reporter turned to the camera and beamed her pretend smile. The operator held up three fingers. Then two. Then one. He pointed toward her.

"Scarlett Steele here. Joining me today—for her first interview ever in an Xtend News Network exclusive—is the High Priestess, Emma Barlow." Scarlett turned to Emma. "Thank you for taking time to talk with me today. There's been some exciting developments with you leading the raid to free the prisoners. Tell our viewers, Emma, what you did to bring this about. Was it a middle-of-the-night incursion?" She thrust the microphone in Emma's face.

"Nothing nearly as dramatic." Emma laughed. "I simply walked up to the front gate and said I was there for the prisoners. The guards released them.

Now we're here at the school, using it as a staging area so we can send everyone home."

"I understand you took a lead role in making this happen."

"To be correct," Emma said, "the Sovereign took the lead. I merely followed."

"What sort of opposition did you face?"

"Very little." Emma nodded to Angie, who stood just out of the shot. "Angie and I cast the demons from that evil prison and declared it to be a safe place, a sanctuary. That's when I walked up to the main gate and said I was there to get the prisoners. Then we left. That's all there is to it."

"I have it on good authority that your boyfriend, Joshua Hart, was one of the prisoners. How relieved were you to be reunited with him again? Was it a sweet reunion?"

Emma looked away. "He didn't make it."

"Do you mean he's still at the prison?"

"No," Emma clarified. "I mean, he didn't make it. Shortly before I walked up to the front gate, we heard gunshots. We later learned that Joshua had been hit. He died." Emma tried to blink back her tears but was unsuccessful.

That's when Angie jumped in front of the camera and pulled the microphone to her. "Please give the High Priestess some privacy. This is a difficult time for her, having lost someone so close. She's not had any time to grieve his loss because she's focusing on getting all these people home. Like any great leader, she's putting their needs before her own."

As Angie spoke, Emma slid out of the shot. The camera operator panned to follow Emma but then jerked back to Scarlett when the reporter resumed talking. "I'm so sorry, High Priestess. We didn't know." Then her pretend smile popped back on her face, more freaky than ever. "I know the High Priestess will want to complete our interview once she regains her composure. We will resume shortly. Until then, back to you, John."

The red light on the camera went dark, and the operator lowered the device. That's when Barney rushed up in a rage. "How dare you do this!" he yelled at Scarlett. "You were completely out of line and behaved unprofessionally. This is not the deal I agreed to. I see it was a mistake to offer the exclusive to Xtend News Network. Rest assured, I won't make that error again."

"I was just trying to get an interesting story for our audience," Scarlett said. "It was a mistake. I'm sorry."

"I'm going to make sure your career is over."

"But I keep saying I'm sorry. What else can I do?"

Barney continued berating Scarlett, and she continued trying to salvage the situation. Before long, Scarlett was crying, too, just like Emma.

Angie moved over to Emma to offer comfort, putting her arm around the quaking teenager. "She was completely out of line and should never have asked those questions."

Emma shook her head. "She didn't know about Joshua and was just trying to do her job. But she caught me off guard. I didn't know what to say."

That's when Angie did the exact thing Emma longed for. The kind nurse took Emma's hand in hers. That's when Angie said the exact thing Emma wanted to hear, even though it was a lie. "It's going to be all right."

That's when Emma completely broke down, sobbing uncontrollably.

Angie guided the trembling teen further away from the people, toward the van and around behind it. With Joshua's corpse inside, no one would dare bother them there.

Through her tears, Emma tried to read a text

message she just received. It was blurry. She handed her phone to Angie.

"It's from your mom. She says, 'I just heard your interview and am so sorry. I know you don't like to use the phone, but if you want to talk, call me. Please.'" Angie looked up at Emma and brushed the hair out of Emma's face. "Would you like me to send her a response?"

"I so wish she was here," Emma said. "Tell her I'll try to call later."

Emma brushed her eyes and blinked a few times. She dragged her shirtsleeve over her cheek and sniffled.

Angie sent the message. When she handed Emma's phone back to her, the screen was no longer blurry.

"Where are you?" came Mom's text response. "I'll get there as soon as I can."

"We're in Lakeview County," Emma texted back. "Wherever that is. I just know it's several hours from home."

A couple minutes later, Emma's mom responded with a text. "If we leave now, your father and I can get there by midnight."

"Thanks," Emma texted back. "But if everything works out, I should be on my way home by then. Hope to see you Sunday."

"Remember," came mom's text response, "you can call me. Anytime."

"Got it! Thanks!!!" Emma slid her phone back into her pocket.

Just then another text came in.

It was Chloe. "So sorry, girlfriend. What can I do?"

"You can pray." Emma texted. "Maybe the whole gang can."

Emma waited for Chloe to respond. But she didn't. Instead, a video call came in.

Emma connected, and Chloe's comforting smile greeted her. Seeing her BFF soothed her still unprocessed grief. "Long distance hug," Chloe said. She extended her left hand—the one not holding her phone—around it as if hugging Emma.

Emma received the hug with appreciation. "Back at ya." Emma returned the gesture to Chloe.

"I so appreciate your video. It means the world to me. Mom can text and call, but she doesn't like to video. But seeing your smiling face is almost as good."

"Normally I'd be offended." Chloe smirked. "But given the circumstances, I understand."

"Where are you?" Emma said, wanting to change the subject. "What's all the commotion?"

"We got too crowded in the communications office and moved to our classroom."

"We? It sounds like you have an army there."

"So much communication came in because of your videos. Beatrice couldn't begin to keep up. So we called for reinforcements. All your disciples are here, and we're cranking away at the messages. Kayla's even talking on the phone. Can you believe it?"

"Kayla? The girl hardly talks at all."

"She had a slow start but is embracing it. She's getting quite good. And she even talked Natalie into helping."

"I didn't mean to cause extra work." Emma sighed. "What types of messages are you getting?"

"Some people are having trouble with the new pages on the website. Others have questions beyond what we posted. Lots just want to say they're praying for you and all the prisoners, for your safe return. And many are donating money. I guess that's how they feel they can best help, even though you didn't ask for donations."

"Please thank everyone for me. I'm encouraged just knowing what you're doing."

"Will do!"

Emma couldn't think what to say next. She was drained, emotionally, physically, and spiritually. She checked her aura in the spiritual realm. It was dangerously low. She'd need to recharge soon by sitting in the Sovereign's presence. But she didn't know how soon that would be. Then she recalled the time her body collapsed because she didn't get the spiritual rest she needed.

Chloe broke the long silence. "I guess I should get back to work. But I'm available whenever you want. Anytime. Day or night."

"Love you!"

"Back at ya. Bye."

Once the video ended, Emma's emotions erupted again. She prayed for the Sovereign to give her strength . . . and composure.

Emma didn't know how long she stood there trying to get a grip on herself, but when she had mostly regained control of her emotions, Barney walked up. "I apologize profusely for what happened. That should have never occurred. Rest assured, the interview is over, and that reporter is permanently barred from ever talking to you again."

## 19

# TESTIMONY

Emma shook her head. "Thank you for protecting me, but I must finish the interview."

"Why?" came Barney's incredulous reply.

"If I don't, the last thing the people will have seen is the High Priestess having a meltdown on national TV. Though I don't care what they think of me, I do care what they think about the Sovereign. I must be a good representative. That's why I need to finish the interview."

"Are you sure?"

"Yes. But questions about Joshua are off-limits."

Barney looked at Angie. The nurse shrugged. "If Emma wants it, that's what we should do."

Barney huffed. "Then I'll make it happen.

Please stand by while I patch things up—to make lemonade out of lemons, as they say."

That's when Emma noticed Scarlett behind the news van. She sat on the ground, with her head in her hands, shoulders shaking.

Emma edged up to the repentant reporter. "Mind if I join you?" Scarlett looked up. The sight of the young woman's tearstained cheeks reminded Emma of her own appearance. She used her shirtsleeve to dab at her own eyes.

Scarlett nodded. "Again, let me say how very sorry I am. I completely blew it. You have every reason to hate me."

"I don't hate you," Emma said. "I want to make sure you're okay. When you're ready, we can complete the interview."

Scarlett shook her head. "No. We can't. They just fired me."

Emma reached out to Scarlett. "Once they see how brilliantly you wrap up our interview, they're sure to take you back."

"This was my chance. My one chance. It was my first national broadcast, and I blew it. And you paid the price for my selfishness."

"Let's put this all behind us," Emma said, "and move ahead."

When Scarlett looked at Emma, her smile was genuine—for the first time. Everything would work out. Emma knew it.

After half an hour, Scarlett and Emma were ready to complete the interview. Questions about Joshua were off-limits. This time there'd be no handheld mic to move between them. Instead, they were each fitted with their own lapel microphone to allow for a more natural conversation.

Scarlett redid her makeup, following Emma's advice that less was more. This time they sat in chairs and under a shade tree. This time it wouldn't be an overeager reporter trying to make a name for herself and an unsuspecting subject unprepared to answer an impossible question. It would be more like two friends—albeit new ones—sharing their personal conversation with the rest of the country.

The camera operator again gave them a count-down and pointed to Scarlett to begin.

"Scarlett Steele here with Xtend News Network for part two of my exclusive interview with Emma Barlow. Emma, let me say on behalf of myself, our entire news team, and the rest of the country how sorry we are to hear of your loss. Please accept our sincere condolences."

"Thank you," Emma said.

"It's quite remarkable how you led your team here and followed the Sovereign's leading to get the prisoners released. We covered that in part one of our interview. What we haven't addressed is what brought you to this point. Tell our viewers about your spiritual journey. Take as much time as you need." Scarlett's relaxed nature and unpretentious smile put Emma at ease.

"It all started a few months ago. I began studying the Holy Text each night in secret. I didn't tell anyone, because I was taught that normal people can't read the Holy Text."

"That's certainly what I heard," Scarlett said. "Is everyone wrong?"

"Let's say they're misinformed, but I can assure you that that teaching is not true. Scripture is for everyone. History 2.14 says so. We need only read it. The Divine Spirit can guide us. Then we do what it says. It's that simple."

"For beginners like me, where should we start?"

Emma beamed at the question. "For most people, I'd say to first read the History section. For those who enjoy poetic language or seek inspiration, read the Wisdom section. But save Prophecy for later."

"Got it! History or Wisdom first. Prophecy last.

What impact did reading the Holy Text have on you?"

"As I read and studied it," Emma said, "I sensed the Sovereign's presence in all I did, every day. My life took on new meaning. I felt a drive to do something more, even though I didn't understand it. I began seeing the Divine's hand at work all around me—and in me."

"I'd certainly like that too," Scarlett said. "How did you respond to . . . to this spiritual yearning? What did you do?"

"I knew how badly we needed a new High Priest to lead our people. I also knew that everyone who had tried to approach the Sovereign ended up either dead or deranged. Yet, I knew I needed to try."

Scarlett gasped. "Weren't you afraid the same thing would happen to you?"

"I was, but if I died trying, I would have at least tried. Plus, I'd spend eternity in heaven with the Sovereign. Either way, it would be good."

"What did you do?"

Emma glowed as she recalled what had happened. "I planned to go to the Temple to beg the Sovereign to send us a new High Priest. Yet the

SWAT team tried to stop me. They even arrested me. But the Sovereign helped me escape—"

"What! How did that happen?"

"I was handcuffed between two guards in the back of the SWAT van. The van came to a stop—I assume for a traffic light. The Sovereign told me to lift my hands. When I did, both cuffs fell off. The guards had their eyes closed and didn't notice—I think they were sleeping. I crept out of the van and just walked away."

"That's incredible!" Scarlett's eyes popped wide open. "Actually, amazing would be a better word. What next?"

"The Sovereign spoke words into my mind, telling me where to go and what to do. It took hours, but I eventually wound my way to the Temple. I spent the night locked inside and sought the Sovereign. And if I failed, I was ready to die."

"Since you're here today, we know you didn't die . . . thankfully." Scarlett smiled. "Tell us what happened inside the Temple."

"In the middle of the night, my spirit left my body and ascended into heaven. I thought I was dead. But I wasn't. I was just visiting. The Sovereign shocked me by saying that I was to be the new High

Priest. Then my spirit left heaven and returned to my body."

"I'd like to hear more about this, but I don't want to get us off track from your story. What happened next?"

"In the morning," Emma continued, "when the priests opened the Temple doors, everyone was shocked I survived the night. The priests bowed before me, and the people said my face glowed. Again, the SWAT team tried to stop me, which is a story for another time. The short version is that they failed, and I became the new High Priest that day, the first High Priestess. It was a job I never asked for and didn't want, but each day I rely on the Sovereign to help me do what I need to do to bring about the reforms our religion so desperately needs."

"That's such an inspiring story!" Scarlett beamed. "And it all began with you reading the Holy Text."

## 20

## PARTING WORDS

With the interview over, Emma gave Scarlett a grateful hug. Then Emma sought the person in charge of the news team. She assumed he was the director or something.

"Will Scarlett be able to keep her job?" Emma asked.

"Given your most excellent second interview, that won't be a problem."

"Good news," Emma said. "Second question. She said you paid for an exclusive. What's that mean?"

"We paid a fee to interview you and be the only news team invited to cover these events."

"That doesn't seem right," Emma said.

"It's common practice in matters such as this," the director explained.

"How much?"

"Half a million, exactly what Mr. Clark demanded."

Emma gasped. "I don't feel right about it. You may keep the money."

"We've already made the payment to the Temple as specified. It's a done deal."

"Thank you," Emma said. "If you're interested, Scarlett can do a follow-up interview with me when I get back and have had time to recover from all that's happened. No charge."

"I accept your generous offer, but we have more seasoned reporters with greater experience. Scarlett was involved today only because she was the most available."

"I prefer Scarlett. I think we have a good connection."

"Then I accept," the director said. "Should I contact Mr. Clark to set up the arrangements?"

"I'll have him contact you when I'm ready, but don't let him shake you down for any more money."

"Agreed, High Priestess." The director extended his hand to Emma, and she shook it. "We'll be leaving shortly," he said. "We want to cover the released prisoners as they arrive at the airport and head for home."

"Before you do," Emma said. "I'm about to record another update for social media. If you want to film it for your coverage, that would be fine. Just wait for about half an hour before you air it. Does that work?"

The man agreed.

Emma returned to the table and chairs where she and Scarlett did their second interview. She invited Scarlett to join her, even though the reporter wouldn't take part in Emma's update.

Emma pulled out her phone. She relaxed her shoulders and beamed a smile. Nodding to the camera operator, she pressed record on her phone right as the camera's red light came on.

"Emma Barlow here with another update. We have all the return trips scheduled and have posted the information on our website. Check there to know when your loved ones will return and how they'll be traveling. We'll use buses, trains, and planes. Also, look for the groups to post updates as they travel and when they get home.

"If you see a group of travelers today or tomorrow all wearing orange jumpsuits, please give them your support and encourage them on their journey. The clothes they're wearing are all they have until they get home.

"My bus will be the last one to leave. I plan to give a final update once we return home tomorrow. Thank you for all your prayers and support.

"Oh, one more thing. Look for another interview with me and Scarlett Steele in the next couple of weeks. See you then!"

Emma waved goodbye and stopped the recording.

## 21

### LEAVING AT LAST

E mma gave Scarlett a tight goodbye hug and thanked the camera operator and director for their work. As the news van pulled away, four trucks from the prison arrived with their evening meal. Everyone got in line, following the protocol Hernandez had established for their noon meal. He didn't even need to remind them what to do.

Jerry had kept Emma updated on developments at the prison. There was every indication that the next shift would not be supportive. Several workers promised to drop off nonperishable food items on their way home in a couple of hours. This would provide some food for the people to take with them as they left, as well as feed the remaining people in the morning.

"They've labeled me as the ringleader and blamed me for releasing all the prisoners," Jerry said. "I fully expect they'll fire me. But I'll show them. I'll quit before they can."

Emma felt sorry for the kind man. He had done the right thing and would pay the price for it. She lifted her right hand to bless him. "May the Sovereign protect you, guide you, and provide for your needs."

Once everyone had eaten, the vans pulled away. It wasn't long before three cars returned, loaded with boxes of food. Jerry—along with the other two drivers—had resigned from working at the prison. This protected them from being fired for delivering this last batch of food.

As they drove away, Emma returned her attention to her team's plans to get the people home.

School buses would leave with those going by planes and trains to get them to the terminal or station with a suitable cushion before their scheduled departure—but not too soon.

For those traveling by charter bus, they would leave as each bus arrived, with those traveling the furthest leaving first. Emma's bus, even though they had a good distance to cover, would leave last. This would allow her team time to wrap up everything before they left.

She encouraged the released prisoners to make sure they were leaving the school in good shape before they left. She didn't want to cause any more work for Carli or the school staff than they already had.

Emma suggested they video each bus as it was being loaded. Anyone who wanted could record a brief message for their family and friends. Everyone thought it was a good idea. They took turns with the recordings, sending them back to Chloe and Lane, who remained faithfully working at the Temple into the night.

One member of the ABT airlines logistics team rode the first bus to the airport to guide the passengers of each bus as it arrived. The other member rode the first bus to the train station. Only their leader remained. She left late that evening but only after reviewing the last few details with Christopher. He would be point going forward.

By midnight, most of the people had left. Only six groups remained. Two had Sunday morning flights and one would go by train at noon. The other three were on buses, which would arrive early the next morning.

Angie eased up to Emma. "You're pushing yourself too hard. You need to recharge your spirit. We don't want another repeat of last week."

"I know," Emma said. "But we're all pushing ourselves hard."

"If one of us falters, the rest can cover," Angie said. "But as our leader, we need you alert and at your best. You must rest."

"There's too much to do. I can't."

"Do I have to call your mother?"

Emma laughed. "I don't think you need to. You're filling in for her just fine." Emma gave Angie a friendly pat on her upper arm.

Then Emma headed to the Temple van. It was the best place for her to go and not be interrupted. Though the thought of being alone with Joshua's dead body filled her with unease, the Sovereign confirmed Emma should indeed retreat to the van. Before long, she basked in the Sovereign's presence to recharge her spirit. She soon drifted asleep.

She dreamed of being in heaven with the Sovereign, dazzled by the Almighty's bright, blinding light.

The Sovereign whispered, *Joshua is sleeping. Go wake him.*

*He's dead,* Emma responded. *Angie confirmed it. I saw his body. We all did.*

*Joshua is sleeping. Go wake him,* the Sovereign repeated.

*I can't.*

*Joshua is sleeping,* the Sovereign said a third time. *Go wake him.*

Emma opened her eyes and stretched. It was morning, and her bus had just arrived.

## 22

### HEADING HOME

After thanking Carli for her support and use of the school and buses, Emma videoed another update, but not before wiping the sleep from her eyes and checking her appearance. For not having showered since Friday morning, she didn't look too bad.

She relaxed her frame, rolled her shoulders back, and pressed record. "It's Sunday morning here at the school," she whispered, as if someone might be sleeping. "I'm about to board the last bus. Please pray for our safety—for everyone's safety—as we head home. And be sure to watch today's service online. We've prepared a special message. Thanks to technology, I'll take part remotely . . . from our bus as we drive down the road. See you soon, my friends."

Emma stopped the recording, posted it on social media, and boarded the bus. She was the last to do so. She plopped down next to Mrs. Butler.

"I've been praying for your release ever since we heard you were arrested and sent for retraining," Emma said. "I fully expected the Sovereign to answer my prayers for you and the other prisoners, but I never thought I'd be involved."

"When Joshua told me you were the new High Priestess," Mrs. Butler said, "I was surprised, but it makes perfect sense. Last year in class, you stood above everyone else in how well you grasped Scripture. You absorbed everything like a sponge, more so than any student I've ever had."

"Are you excited to get back to teaching?"

"I'm not going back. I'll tender my resignation." Before Emma could ask why, Mrs. Butler explained. "I love teaching the Holy Text, but since it's a public school, I'm prohibited from talking about faith or application. So I'm going to look for a new job where I have the freedom to teach about faith."

Emma perked up. "Maybe you can teach at the Temple," she said. "We already decided to add religion to our curriculum. You could teach us! And we're working on reopening the Temple school to train new priests. You could definitely help with that. Then there are the current priests. They didn't learn anything about the Holy Text in seminary, but they're hungry to learn." Emma paused to catch her breath.

Mrs. Butler's face glowed. "What would you think about me also holding evening classes for adults?"

"Great idea! In person or online?"

"How about both?"

"Won't that make you way too busy?" Emma asked.

"You had me first hour last year, so you know I'm not a morning person. It would be ideal if I could start my day at about ten or eleven each morning and work till seven or eight in the evening. That'd be a perfect rhythm for me."

"When do you want to start?"

"How about Monday? But don't I need to be interviewed first?"

"We can skip that step," Emma said. "Consider yourself hired. I'll text Frederick and Jennifer to let them know."

Peace flooded Mrs. Butler's face. Her eyelids

fluttered as a smile formed. "Thank you!" she mouthed. "Thank you so much."

"You're welcome," Emma said. "If you'll excuse me, I need to get ready for my part in today's service."

Fred, Mark, and Emma had already planned for Emma to offer the opening greeting live for each service. But she wouldn't teach; Mark would do that. Then she'd give the concluding blessing.

Emma moved to the front of the bus and announced what she would be doing. The passengers would be in the background of her shot. Turning around, she grabbed the edge of the seat for support with her left hand and held her phone out in her right. The video feed was already going. The plan was to display her on the overhead in the sanctuary when it was her turn.

She received her cue. "Welcome to today's service! I wish I was with you in person, but as you likely know, something came up. I'm riding the bus back to the Temple right now. We have a busload of wrongly imprisoned people who are eager to get home. We expect to arrive around dusk. I'll share the message I was working on with you next Sunday. It's about Talia, the young girl who led the army to victory when none of the men would. But for today, hear these words from the Holy Text: 'Free the prisoners, heal the sick, wake the dead, and proclaim the Sovereign throughout all the nations.' This is from Prophecy 17.3. Mark will teach on this today."

She stopped recording and lowered her phone. When she turned around, the passengers applauded.

Nearly an hour later, Emma repeated the process to give the service's closing blessing. This time Mrs. Butler held her phone, leaving Emma with both hands free. In grand fashion, she reached out to the people in the sanctuary.

"Receive this blessing. May the Sovereign go with you everywhere you go. May the Almighty protect you in everything you do. And may the Divine Spirit speak to you as you read the Holy Text. So be it." Emma flashed an inviting smile and waved at the camera. Mrs. Butler moved around Emma to focus on the people riding the bus. They, too, waved their goodbyes.

Emma repeated both parts for the second service.

## 23

---

## AN EVENTFUL TRIP

Having eaten what little food they had on the bus, everyone was hungry. Around one o'clock, the driver pulled off the highway and stopped at a fast-food court. Topher and Christopher planned to use their Temple credit cards to pay for everyone's meals, but each restaurant refused to accept payment. They wanted to do their part to help the released prisoners get home.

Emma felt she'd done all she could to lead the people. Now she could focus on herself; at last she could mourn Joshua's death. After gobbling her food, Emma headed to the van. She planned to ride with Joshua's body the rest of the way.

*If only I knew how to grieve.*

But instead of getting in the van, Emma walked

to the back. She opened the rear doors. It may have been her imagination, but she was sure a foul stench wafted out. She stared at the body bag that held his shell, in shock at the stark reality that Joshua was dead.

The Sovereign's words formed inside her mind. *Look inside.*

Emma hesitated and then unzipped the body bag. She gasped. His body looked even worse than before.

*Wake him*, came the Sovereign's words.

*I can't*, Emma replied. *He's not sleeping. He's dead.*

*Just as it's easy for you to wake a sleeping person, so it is for me to raise someone from the dead.*

*Then you do it!*

*No*, the Sovereign shot back. *Take a step of faith and do it yourself. Trust me for the outcome.*

Emma closed her eyes and inhaled slowly. She had faith the Almighty could restore life to Joshua, but she clung to only a small grain of that belief. And she could barely hang on to that. *I do believe! Cover my unbelief.*

She looked down at Joshua. "In the name of the Almighty Sovereign, I command you, Joshua Hart, to open your eyes, inhale life, and rise."

Nothing happened. Emma's grip on what little

belief she had slowly slipped away. Yet her feet remained anchored to that spot as she fixed her gaze on Joshua's corpse.

When she had given up all hope, Joshua's eyelids fluttered. His chest rose as he took in oxygen. It was a shallow breath, but it was a start. Four more slow breaths followed, each one stronger than the one before. Then he opened his eyes, looked at Emma, and sat up.

Emma squealed. She wrapped her arms around him, planting a kiss on his cheek. "Joshua! You're alive!"

"It's all because of you," Joshua said.

"And the Sovereign," Emma added.

When they pulled away from each other, Joshua waved his hand in front of his nose. "What stinks? It's really rank."

"It's you, silly."

He nodded and shimmied out of the body bag. He gave her a kiss on the lips. This time she kissed him back, like she should've done the first time.

"We should call your parents," Emma said, "and let them know you're no longer dead."

"I don't have my phone."

Emma handed hers to him.

"I don't know their number. It's in speed dial."

"I don't have it either," Emma said. Then she brightened. "But I do have your sister's." She grabbed her phone back from Joshua to video Sarah.

"Emma!" Sarah shrieked. "It's so good to see you!" With a sniff, Sarah rubbed at her red-rimmed eyes. "I'm so confused. I knew, that I knew, that I knew, that Joshua would be all right. The Sovereign promised me. But he died anyway. What's up with that?"

Emma waited for Sarah to go on, but the young girl didn't. This was the least Emma had ever heard her say in a single breath. "Good news!" Emma beamed as a tear trickled down her cheek. She rotated the phone and pointed the screen at Joshua.

"Hi, sis." Joshua waved.

"Joshua!" Sarah screamed. "Mom. Dad. Come quick. It's Joshua. He's alive!"

Joshua took the phone from Emma, and she stepped away to give him time with his family. That's when she noticed several people who'd witnessed the whole thing. They stood there with eyes wide open and jaws agape in disbelief . . . and joy.

Angie and Mrs. Butler rushed up and enveloped Emma in a three-way hug. Soon everyone gathered around them, amazed at what the Sovereign had done. When Joshua walked up, they parted to let him in. That's when Emma noticed his torn and bloodstained jumpsuit; she realized that Mrs. Butler's wasn't blood-soaked but new.

"There's a clean jumpsuit under the body bag," Mrs. Butler said. "I put it there. Aside from the legs being way too short, the rest should fit."

"How? Why? When?" Emma's questions spewed forth.

"After you healed me, Jerry went to get me a fresh jumpsuit. But he didn't know what size to get, so he grabbed two. I changed into one. Without thinking, I tossed the other one on Joshua's body bag. When we transferred his body to the van, I moved the jumpsuit too. I don't know why I did it, but I did."

"Maybe the Sovereign prompted you."

"Perhaps."

Some of the people surrounding them thought so too. Their initial excitement over Joshua's miracle, however, gave way to their desire to get home. They filed back onto the bus. With everyone's approval, Emma rode in the van with Joshua. They had much to cover and needed time to themselves.

She apologized to him for their argument, and

he received it. He apologized to her, and she said he'd done nothing wrong. She extended her hand to his. He wrapped his hand around hers, giving her a gentle squeeze.

Emma gazed into his eyes. Their beautiful brown filled her with delight. He was so handsome. "I just wish you'd have told me what you were doing before you left," she said. "I could've said goodbye and blessed you."

"You'd have just tried to talk me out of it."

He was right. "But why wouldn't you let my spirit connect to yours when I reached out to you?"

"I didn't want to hear your disapproval."

He was right, again. "But you allowed me to connect for a few seconds when you were trying to free the prisoners."

"I wanted you to see what we were doing."

Emma sighed. "Then when I told you to be careful, you shut me out. I guess I deserved that. Sorry."

"I've already forgiven you. Let's move on."

Emma rested her other hand on top of his. He placed his free hand over hers. There was nothing more to say.

He was alive. They were together. Their future

awaited. That's when she knew it. *Everything would be okay.*

At last, Emma's bliss over being reunited gave way to fatigue. She leaned into him and fell asleep. It wasn't until the van slowed down to turn into the Temple grounds that she woke up.

A throng of well-wishers greeted them: family, friends, and those who just wanted to witness their homecoming.

Joshua raced up to his family, while Emma ran to hers. She hugged her mom first, next her dad, and then Hailey. Even the more reserved Brayden wormed in for his hug.

It was good to be back and reunited with her family, to be home.

## 24

## CELEBRATE

After a good night's sleep, Emma joined the priests for breakfast in the cafeteria. They listened with excitement as she shared everything about her trip to free the prisoners. Then she hustled off to school, where she sat next to Joshua for the first time since they'd been doing school together at the Temple. Chloe sat on her other side. Lane and Kayla joined them.

They also wanted to hear about all that had happened. Jennifer allowed them to skip some of their lessons to celebrate what the Sovereign had done. Tomorrow they'd return to schoolwork in earnest.

At noon, Emma headed to the cafeteria to have

her regular working lunch with her team. They, too, had questions.

After she filled them in, Barney surprised Emma with exciting news. "As you requested, High Priestess, I reached out to Scarlett Steele about a possible follow-up so you could share what happened with Joshua. It turns out she grew up in the area and was already on her way home to visit her parents. That means she's in town and will be available this afternoon at two. Assuming that's agreeable to you."

"Of course it is," Emma replied. "Thanks for making it happen."

An hour and a half later, Emma and Joshua walked into the small meeting room in the palace. Barney followed. There waited Scarlett and a cameraman.

The pert reporter withdrew at the sight of Barney, and he scowled at her.

"It might be best," Emma said to Barney, "if you wait outside during the interview."

"Though I think it unwise, I will comply with your request." He spun around and stomped off.

Emma hugged Scarlett like a long-lost friend. Then Emma introduced Joshua. The three discussed the interview, while the cameraman helped them with their mics.

They sat in a semicircle, with Emma in the middle and Scarlett to her left. Joshua sat on her right. The cameraman zoomed in on Scarlett. He cued her.

"Scarlett Steele here with Xtend News Network. I'm excited to have this special encore interview with our High Priestess, Emma Barlow. She has an amazing update to share. I want you to be the first to hear it."

The camera pulled out to include Emma in the shot with Scarlett.

The reporter continued, "Emma, just two days ago, the entire country found out that your boyfriend, Joshua Hart, was killed in the prison before he could be released and reunited with you. Please update our viewers on what happened the next day."

Emma could hardly contain herself. "Joshua was dead for over a day, sealed in a body bag. But on Sunday afternoon the Sovereign raised him from the dead, just like we read about in the Holy Text. It's a miracle! I'm pleased to announce that Joshua is alive again . . . and well. He's here with us right now."

With this as his cue, the cameraman zoomed out further to include all three of them in the shot. Though not planned, Emma and Joshua's hands found each other and their fingers intertwined.

"Joshua, let me welcome you back from the dead," Scarlett said. "Tell us exactly what happened."

"My religion teacher, Mrs. Butler, and I—"

"Wait just a second!" Scarlett brightened and leaned in. "Your religion teacher is Mrs. Butler? At Riverside High? I had her when I went to school there!"

"Yes, Mrs. Butler from Riverside High. She'd been arrested for heresy and was sent to the prison for retraining. As soon as I arrived, she shared with me her plans to escape. But she needed help to pull it off. I agreed. On Saturday morning, we both felt peace flood into the prison. At the time, we didn't know what caused it, but we were sure the Sovereign was at work. We took it as a sign for us to move forward with her escape plan." Joshua paused to focus his thoughts.

"Mrs. Butler had gotten ahold of two keycards. We used them to unlock our cell doors. Then we ran down the corridor, unlocking everyone else's. When we finished the first corridor and turned into the second one, two guards charged at us with guns. They fired. We were both hit."

Scarlett interrupted again. "Hold on. Mrs. Butler was shot too? Please tell me she's okay. Will she recover?"

"Mrs. Butler was hit twice but is now okay," Emma said. "At the Sovereign's prompting, I commanded the bullets to come out of her body and then healed her wounds. She's fine."

"What a relief!" Scarlett said.

"But that's when I learned Joshua was dead," Emma added.

"I'm so sorry," Scarlett said. "I'm also sorry for interrupting you, Joshua. Take us back to the moment you were hit. Were you in great pain?"

Joshua shook his head. "I guess I was in shock. As they wheeled me to the infirmary, I felt life slipping away. My body went numb, and everything turned black. I stopped breathing. I knew I'd soon die."

"You were aware of all this?" Scarlett leaned forward. "Amazing. What happened next?"

"My spirit left my body. It was a smooth parting. I floated, rising into heaven. I went faster and faster. Above blazed a bright light coming from the center of heaven. It blinded me. It shone from the Sovereign. I spent the next day in the Sovereign's presence, at peace and fully loved. It was total peace, pure and holy. I never knew it was possible to feel that way. I can't explain it any better."

"I appreciate you sharing the best you could," Scarlett said. "I think we can all agree that heaven's a wondrous place. Did you know your body would be raised back to life?"

"The Sovereign wasn't clear about that, merely saying that I might return—or I might not. It was up to Emma."

Emma gasped. "I had no idea." She squeezed his hand.

"This whole time," Joshua continued, "I watched what was happening on earth. I saw what Emma did to lead all the people to safety. I also felt what she felt. In a way, I experienced the grief she carried over my death. Though I wanted to stay in heaven with the Sovereign, I didn't want to leave Emma alone or for her to suffer."

"I can attest to just how badly she was hurting over your death," Scarlett said. "What happened next?"

"From heaven I watched Emma go to the back

of the van where my body lay. At the exact moment she opened the doors, my spirit eased out of heaven. I said goodbye to the Sovereign—for now.

"As my spirit rushed back to earth to reunite with my body, I heard Emma say, 'In the name of the Almighty Sovereign, I command you, Joshua Hart, to open your eyes, inhale life, and rise.' I felt my eyelids flutter and oxygen flood into my lungs. That's when I regained control of my body. I sat up and gave Emma a hug."

"That's so remarkable." Scarlett dabbed her right eye. "Thank you for sharing this with us today. We're so touched by your experience and encouraged by the Sovereign's power. We also see just how much you love each other. How long have you been dating?"

Emma laughed. "We've never been on a date."

"What! Why is that?" Scarlett asked.

"For one, I've been too busy in my new role as High Priestess. Another is that neither of us is old enough to drive."

"That would certainly present a problem," Scarlett said. "But you are a couple, right? How long have you been together?"

"I guess about a month," Emma said. "Joshua

had been interested in me before that, but it took a while to realize I liked him too. That wasn't until after I became High Priestess."

"I understand you two hatched the plan for Joshua to go undercover as a prisoner to determine the prison location and free everyone."

"Actually," Joshua said, "we had a bit of a disagreement about that."

Emma interjected. "It wasn't a disagreement. We had a fight. I was a total turd."

Joshua nodded. "Yep, she was a bit of a turd."

Scarlett snickered. "A total turd? That's . . . colorful language. Might you be a little hard on yourself?"

"No," Emma said. "I was a jerk and tried to tell him what to do. I even commanded him to not go. Can you believe it? But I learned my lesson and won't make that mistake again."

"Obviously, you two have moved past that and are in a good place now," Scarlet said. "What do you attribute that to?"

"It's all because of the Sovereign," Joshua said.

"For sure, we trust the Sovereign with everything," Emma added, "our relationship, our lives, and our future."

If you enjoyed *Freeing the Prisoners,* please leave a review online. Your review will help others learn about this book and encourage them to read it too.

Thank you.

## FIGHTING THE FANATICS

BOOK 6 OF THE NEXT HIGH PRIEST SERIES

## Chapter 1: Back to Normal?

At noon, Emma trudged off to lunch, an uncharacteristic scowl on her face. School had not gone well—not at all. The comfortable rhythm she, Chloe, and Joshua enjoyed had evaporated with the addition of Lane and Kayla. It was sure to get worse when her remaining eight disciples joined them later in the week.

School had taken longer than usual, and Emma had to rush through her assignments to finish by lunch.

*Was adding my friends a bad idea? How can I fix this?*

Shuffling along with her was Chloe on her right and Joshua on her left. Lane and Kayla held back, likely sensing they were the reason school had gone so poorly.

Already holding her boyfriend's hand, Emma reached out to clasp Chloe's. "Sovereign Lord," she prayed, "please show us how to move forward with school. Fill us with your peace and give me insight in all I do this afternoon. I ask this for your honor and your kingdom."

Her friends agreed in unison. "Amen." The three of them walked in silence the rest of the way to the cafeteria.

Mechanically, Emma piled food on her tray in the food line and joined her team for their regular working lunch. They were all waiting. Emma tried to shove aside her frustration over the morning to embrace the potential of the afternoon.

She sat down but didn't eat. Instead, she made eye contact with each person. She needed to get their attention before she shared from her heart.

"I so value each one of you and all you do to serve the Sovereign and help me. I don't thank you often enough. Sorry."

"Emma," her dad said, "you do a great job at communicating your appreciation." He paused and looked intently into her eyes. "What's wrong?"

"School was a bit frustrating this morning." Emma blinked back tears. "I'm trying to push that behind me to focus on you and our work here." She took in a slow breath as she reoriented herself. "I've not heard any updates for a few days. Let's do a lightning round. Who wants to go first?"

With hesitation, her dad raised his hand a few inches. It looked funny, but she suppressed her laughter. Instead, she nodded.

"Everything at the health clinic is exceeding my expectations. We've addressed the backlog of staff healthcare concerns and now have extra time. I suggest expanding the clinic to include the priests too."

Fred, her executive administrator, chimed in. "The healthcare coverage the priests have is the best money can buy. We can slash costs in half if we move them to a more typical coverage. The clinic can address what the new plan doesn't cover."

"I've run the numbers," Topher added, "and we'll save enough on the priests' insurance to add coverage for all the staff."

"Everyone agree?" Emma scanned her team. "Let's do it. How long will it take?"

Fred glanced at Emma's father.

"We're ready anytime," her dad confirmed.

"The smoothest transition," Fred said, "will be to start the beginning of next month. I'll make it happen."

Emma glanced at Christopher, who oversaw human resources. "I've completed doing the competitive wage analysis," he said, "and recommend moving forward with phase one of staff raises. It will mean moving everyone from minimum wage to a higher base. Then, in phase two, we can begin moving individual staff to their competitive level."

Emma's eyes darted to their accountant. "I ran the numbers on that too," Topher said. "I agree we can move forward on phase one with no problem. It will be sustainable."

Emma nodded. "Let's do it," she said to Christopher.

Topher continued his update. "A massive flood of donations came in over the weekend while you were securing the release of the prisoners. It's a record by far and nearly overwhelmed our servers. Anyway, we should be able to move forward with your plans to renovate the old dorm rooms and reopen the Temple school. I recommend we allocate those funds toward that purpose. I'll work on getting repair estimates."

That's when Mark interjected. "Another area needing capital improvements is the ancient Temple. Ezra is working on some exciting ideas."

Emma sighed. "And I was hoping to renovate the old auditorium."

"Toward what end?" Fred asked.

Emma shrugged. "Not sure. But the Sovereign told me to get it ready to put back into service—soon."

"It would be unwise to pursue all three projects at once," Fred said. "Let's contemplate this and revisit it tomorrow."

Everyone agreed, and all but Emma left to return to work.

Emma remained seated. She pushed her tray of untouched food aside and lowered her forehead to rest on the table. She knew she should be happy—overjoyed, actually—for all the forward progress on the Temple reforms she was spearheading, but she wasn't. At this moment, it all overwhelmed her. She tried to pray but couldn't even focus enough to do that.

That's when Barney cleared his throat. During the whole lunch, her aide had stood in the periphery, available if she needed him to do anything. His emotional support dog, Montgomery, snuggled around his shoe.

Emma sat up with a start.

"Mr. Hernandez approaches, High Priestess. I suspect he has an update."

Emma stood to welcome Hernandez but almost toppled.

"Perhaps you should eat something," Barney advised.

She sat and chomped into a roll as she motioned for Hernandez to join her.

But before he did, he looked at Barney. "I have a personal update for Emma," he said. "Will you please give us privacy?"

Barney scowled but said nothing. With a huff, he turned and marched away, parking himself at the far end of the cafeteria where he could watch Emma.

Hernandez sat across from her. He leaned forward. "You'll never believe what I found on my jacket when we got back on Sunday," he whispered. He pulled a small vial from his pocket, sheltered in his hands so only Emma could see.

A small device lay on the bottom of the container.

"What is it?"

"It's an electronic listening device. Someone was eavesdropping on everything I said the entire trip."

Emma gasped. "Who'd do such a thing?"

Continue this story in *Fighting the Fanatics*, Book 6 of The Next High Priest Series.

# ABOUT PETER DEHAAN

Peter DeHaan is an adult who dreams of being a teenager. When he's not contemplating grown-up thoughts, his mind retreats to the domain of invented worlds with his loyal and most real, yet still imaginary, friends. What grand adventures they have: righting wrongs, solving problems, and making their world a better place to live.

His first published adventures come to life in "The Next High Priest Series"—a faith-friendly speculative fiction adventure in a world just like ours . . . only different.

Next up is *The Curious Gift*, a YA contemporary novella with a hint of the supernatural.

Then comes "The Ice Creamed Series," a present-day quest for friendship and love, all the while trying to survive high school unscathed and ping-ponging between responsible impulses and irresponsible slipups.

Want more? Get a free short-story prequel about Emma along with news of upcoming books when you sign up to receive Peter's updates at PeterDeHaan.com/fiction.

# FICTION BOOKS BY PETER DEHAAN

## The Next High Priest Series

*Seeking the Sovereign*

*Confronting the Chaos*

*Dueling the Devil*

*Reforming the Religion*

*Freeing the Prisoners*

*Fighting the Fanatics*

*Perfecting the Priesthood*

*Pursuing the Politicians*

*Restoring the Repentant*

Learn more at PeterDeHaan.com/fiction.